The Amateur Garden

George W. Cable

The Amateur Garden

Copyright © 2020 Bibliotech Press
All rights reserved

The present edition is a reproduction of previous publication of this classic work. Minor typographical errors may have been corrected without note, however, for an authentic reading experience the spelling, punctuation, and capitalization have been retained from the original text.

ISBN: 978-1-64799-384-9

CONTENTS

MY OWN ACRE 1
THE AMERICAN GARDEN 23
WHERE TO PLANT WHAT 44
THE COTTAGE GARDENS OF NORTHAMPTON 60
THE PRIVATE GARDEN'S PUBLIC VALUE 72
THE MIDWINTER GARDENS OF NEW ORLEANS 91

MY OWN ACRE

A lifelong habit of story-telling has much to do with the production of these pages.

All the more does it move me because it has always included, as perhaps it does in most story-tellers, a keen preference for true stories, stories of actual occurrence.

A flower-garden trying to be beautiful is a charming instance of something which a storyteller can otherwise only dream of. For such a garden is itself a story, one which actually and naturally occurs, yet occurs under its master's guidance and control and with artistic effect.

Yet it was this same story-telling bent which long held me back while from time to time I generalized on gardening and on gardens other than my own. A well-designed garden is not only a true story happening artistically but it is one that passes through a new revision each year, "with the former translations diligently compared and revised." Each year my own acre has confessed itself so full of mistranslations of the true text of gardening, has promised, each season, so much fairer a show in its next edition, and has been kept so prolongedly busy teaching and reteaching its master where to plant what, while as to money outlays compelled to live so much more like a poet than like a prince, that the bent for story-telling itself could not help but say wait.

Now, however, the company to which this chapter logically belongs is actually showing excellent reasons why a history of their writer's own acre should lead them. Let me, then, begin by explaining that the small city of Northampton, Massachusetts, where I have lived all the latter three-fifths of my adult years, sits on the first rise of ground which from the west overlooks the alluvial meadows of the Connecticut, nine miles above South Hadley Falls. Close at its back a small stream, Mill River, coming out of the Hampshire hills on its way to the Connecticut, winds through a strip of woods so fair as to have been named—from a much earlier day than when Jenny Lind called it so—"Paradise." On its town side this wooded ground a few hundred yards wide drops suddenly a hundred feet or so to the mill stream and is cut into many transverse ravines.

In its timber growth, conspicuous by their number, tower white-pines, while among them stand only less loftily a remarkable variety of forest trees imperfectly listed by a certain humble authority as "mostly h-oak, h-ellum, and h-ash, with a little 'ickory."

Imperfectly listed, for there one may find also the birch and the beech, the linden, sycamore, chestnut, poplar, hemlock-spruce, butternut, and maple overhanging such pleasant undergrowths as the hornbeam and hop-hornbeam, willows, black-cherry and choke-cherry, dogwood and other cornels, several viburnums, bush maples of two or three kinds, alder, elder, sumach, hazel, witch-hazel, the shadblow and other perennial, fair-blooming, sweet-smelling favorites, beneath which lies a leaf-mould rife with ferns and wild flowers.

From its business quarter the town's chief street of residence, Elm Street, begins a gently winding westerly ascent to become an open high-road from one to another of the several farming and manufacturing villages that use the water-power of Mill River. But while it is still a street there runs from it southerly at a right angle a straight bit of avenue some three hundred yards long—an exceptional length of unbent street for Northampton. This short avenue ends at another, still shorter, lying square across its foot within some seventy yards of that suddenly falling wooded and broken ground where Mill River loiters through Paradise. The strip of land between the woods and this last street is taken up by half a dozen dwellings of modest dignity, whose front shade-trees, being on the southerly side, have been placed not on the sidewalk's roadside edge but on the side next the dwellings and close within their line of private ownership: red, white and post-oaks set there by the present writer when he named the street "Dryads' Green." They are now twenty-one years old and give a good shade which actually falls where it is wanted—upon the sidewalk.

On this green of the dryads, where it intercepts the "avenue" that slips over from the Elm Street trolley-cars, lies, such as it is, my own acre; house, lawn, shrubberies and, at the rear, in the edge of the pines, the study. Back there by the study—which sometimes in irony we call the power-house—the lawn merges into my seven other acres, in Paradise. Really the whole possession is a much humbler one than I find myself able to make it appear in the flattering terms of land measure. Those seven acres of Paradise I acquired as "waste land." Nevertheless, if I were selling that "waste," that "hole in the ground," it would not hurt my conscience, such as it is, to declare that the birds on it alone are worth more than it cost: wood-thrushes and robins, golden orioles, scarlet tanagers, blackbirds, bluebirds, oven-birds, cedar-birds, veeries, vireos, song-sparrows, flycatchers, kinglets, the flicker, the cuckoo, the nuthatch, the chickadee and the rose-breasted grosbeak, not to mention jays or kingfishers, swallows, the little green heron or that cock of the walk, the red squirrel.

Speaking of walks, it was with them—and one drive—in this grove, that I made my first venture toward the artistic enhancement of my acre,—acre this time in the old sense that ignores feet and rods. I was quite willing to make it a matter of as many years as necessary when pursued as play, not work, on the least possible money outlay and having for its end a garden of joy, not of care. By no inborn sagacity did I discover this to be the true first step, but by the trained eye of an honored and dear friend, that distinguished engineer and famous street commissioner of New York, Colonel George E. Waring, who lost his life in the sanitary regeneration of Havana.

"Contour paths" was the word he gave me; paths starting from the top of the steep broken ground and bending in and out across and around its ridges and ravines at a uniform decline of, say, six inches to every ten feet, until the desired terminus is reached below; much as, in its larger way, a railway or aqueduct might, or as cattle do when they roam in the hills. Thus, by the slightest possible interference with natural conditions, these paths were given a winding course every step of which was pleasing because justified by the necessities of the case, traversing the main inequalities of the ground with the ease of level land yet without diminishing its superior variety and charm. And so with contour paths I began to find, right at my back door and on my own acre, in nerve-tired hours, an outdoor relaxation which I could begin, leave off and resume at any moment and which has never staled on me. For this was the genesis of all I have learned or done in gardening, such as it is.

My appliances for laying out the grades were simple enough: a spirit-level, a stiff ten-foot rod with an eighteen-inch leg nailed firmly on one end of it, a twelve-inch leg on the other, a hatchet, and a basket of short stakes with which to mark the points, ten feet apart, where the longer leg, in front on all down grades, rested when the spirit-level, strapped on the rod, showed the rod to be exactly horizontal. Trivial inequalities of surface were arbitrarily cut down or built up and covered with leaves and pine-straw to disguise the fact, and whenever a tree or anything worth preserving stood in the way here came the loaded barrow and the barrowist, like a piece of artillery sweeping into action, and a fill undistinguishable from nature soon brought the path around the obstacle on what had been its lower side, to meander on at its unvarying rate of rise or fall as though nothing—except the trees and wild flowers—had happened since the vast freshets of the post-glacial period built the landscape. I made the drive first, of steeper grade than the paths; but every new length of way built, whether walk or road, made the next easier to build, by making easier going for the artillery, the construction train. Also each new path has made it easier to bring up, for the lawn garden, sand, clay, or leaf-mould, or for hearth consumption all the wood which the grove's natural mortality each year requires to be disposed of. There is a superior spiritual quality in the warmth of a fire of h-oak, h-ash, and even h-ellum gathered from your own acre, especially if the acre is very small and has contour paths. By a fire of my own acre's "dead and down" I write these lines. I never buy cordwood.

Only half the grove has required these paths, the other half being down on the flat margin of the river, traversed by a cart-road at least half a century old, though used by wheels hardly twice a year; but in the three acres where lie the contour paths there is now three-fifths of a mile of them, not a rod of which is superfluous. And then I have two examples of another kind of path: paths with steps; paths which for good and lawful reasons cannot allow you time to go around on the "five per cent" grade but must cut across, taking a single ravine lengthwise, to visit its three fish-pools.

These steps, and two short retaining walls elsewhere in the grove, are made of the field stones of the region, uncut. All are laid "dry" like the ordinary stone fences of New England farms, and the walls are built with a smart inward batter so that the winter frosts may heave them year after year, heave and leave but not tumble them down. I got that idea from a book. Everything worth while on my acre is from books except what two or three professional friends have from time to time dropped into my hungry ear. Both my ears have good appetites—for garden lore.

About half a mile from me, down Mill River, stands the factory of a prized friend who more than any other man helps by personal daily care to promote Northampton's "People's Institute," of whose home-garden work I have much to say in the chapters that follow this one. For forty years or more this factory has been known far and wide as the "Hoe Shop" because it makes shovels. It has never made hoes. It uses water-power, and the beautiful mill-pond behind its high dam keeps the river full back to the rapids just above my own acre. In winter this is the favorite skating-pond of the town and of Smith College. In the greener seasons of college terms the girls constantly pass upstream and down in their pretty rowboats and canoes, making a charming effect as seen from my lawn's rear edge at the head of the pine and oak shaded ravine whose fish-pools are gay by turns with elder, wild sunflower, sumach, iris, water-lilies, and forget-me-not.

This ravine, the middle one of the grove's three, is about a hundred feet wide. When I first began to venture the human touch in it, it afforded no open spot level enough to hold a camp-stool. From the lawn above to the river road below, the distance is three hundred and thirty feet, and the fall, of fifty-five feet, is mostly at the upper end, which is therefore too steep, as well as too full of varied undergrowth, for any going but climbing. In the next ravine on its left there was a clear, cold spring and in the one on its right ran a natural rivulet that trickled even in August; but this middle ravine was dry or merely moist.

Here let me say to any who would try an amateur landscape art on their own acre at the edge of a growing town, that the town's growth tends steadily to diminish the amount of their landscape's natural water supply by catching on street pavements and scores and hundreds of roofs, lawns and walks, and carrying away in sewers, the rain and melting snows which for ages filtered slowly through the soil. Small wonder, I think, that, when in the square quarter-mile between my acre and Elm Street fifty-three dwellings and three short streets took the place of an old farm, my grove, by sheer water famine, lost several of its giant pines. Wonder to me is that the harm seems at length to have ceased.

But about that ravine: one day the nature of its growth and soil, especially its alders, elders, and willows and a show of clay and gravel, forced on my notice the likelihood that here, too, had once been a spring, if no more. I scratched at its head with a stick and out came an imprisoned rill like a recollected word from the scratched head of a schoolboy. Happily the spot was just at the bottom of the impassably steep fall of ground next the edge of the lawn and was almost in the centre of those four acres—one of sward, three of woods—which I proposed to hold under more or less discipline, leaving the rest—a wooded strip running up the river shore—wholly wild, as college girls, for example, would count wildness. In both parts the wealth of foliage on timber and underbrush almost everywhere shut the river out of view from the lawn and kept the eye restless for a glint, if no more, of water. And so there I thought at once to give myself what I had all my life most absurdly wished for, a fish-pool. I had never been able to look upon an aquarium and keep the tenth Commandment. I had never caught a fish without wanting to take it home and legally adopt it into the family—a tendency which once led my son to say, "Yes, he would be pleased to go fishing with me if I would only fish in a sportsmanlike manner." What a beautifully marked fish is the sunperch! Once, in boyhood, I kept six of those "pumpkin-seed" in a cistern, and my smile has never been the same since I lost them—one of my war losses.

I resolved to impound the waters of my spring in the ravine and keep fish at last—without salt—to my heart's content. Yet I remembered certain restraining precepts: first, that law of art which condemns incongruity—requires everything to be in keeping with its natural surroundings—and which therefore, for one thing, makes an American garden the best possible sort of garden to have in America; second, that twin art law, against inutility, which demands that everything in an artistic scheme serve the use it pretends to serve; third, a precept of Colonel Waring's: "Don't fool with running water if you haven't money to fool away"; and, fourth, that best of all gardening rules—look before you leap.

However, on second thought, and tenth, and twentieth, one thought a day for twenty days, I found that if water was to be impounded anywhere on my acre here was the strategic point. Down this ravine, as I have said, was the lawn's one good glimpse of the river, and a kindred gleam intervening would tend, in effect, to draw those farther waters in under the trees and into the picture.

Such relationships are very rewarding to find to whoever would garden well. Hence this mention. One's garden has to do with whatever is in sight from it, fair or otherwise, and it is as feasible and important to plant in the fair as to plant out the otherwise. Also, in making my grove paths, I had noticed that to cross this ravine where at one or two places in its upper half a contour grade would have been pettily circuitous and uninteresting, and to cross it comfortably, there should be either a bridge or a dam; and a dam with water behind it seemed pleasanter every way—showed less incongruity and less inutility—than a bridge with no water under it.

As to "fooling with running water," the mere trickle here in question had to be dragged out of its cradle to make it run at all. It remained for me to find out by experience that even that weakling, imprisoned and grown to a pool, though of only three hundred square feet in surface, when aided and abetted by New England frosts and exposed on a southern slope to winter noonday suns, could give its amateur captor as much trouble—proportionately—as any Hebrew babe drawn from the bulrushes of the Nile is said to have given his.

Now if there is any value in recording these experiences it can be only in the art principles they reveal. To me in the present small instance the principle illustrated was that of the true profile line for ascent or descent in a garden. You may go into any American town where there is any inequality of ground and in half an hour find a hundred or two private lawns graded—from the house to each boundary line—on a single falling curve, or, in plain English, a hump. The best reason why this curve is not artistic, not pleasing, but stupid, is that it is not natural and gains nothing by being unnatural. All gardening is a certain conquest of Nature, and even when "formal" should interfere with her own manner and custom as slightly as is required by the necessities of the case—the needs of that particular spot's human use and joy. The right profile and surface for a lawn of falling grade, the surface which will permanently best beguile both eye and foot, should follow a double curve, an ogee line. For, more or less emphasized, that is Nature's line in all her affable moods on land or water: a descent or ascent beginning gradually, increasing rapidly, and concluding gently. We see it in the face of any smooth knoll or billow. I believe the artists impute to Praxiteles a certain ownership in this double curve. It is a living line; it suggests Nature conscious and astir as no single curve or straight line can.

I admit that even among amateurs this is rather small talk, but it brings me to this point: in the passage of water down a ravine of its own making, this line of Nature astir may repeat itself again and again but is commonly too inaffable, abrupt, angular, to suggest the ogee. In that middle part of it where the descent is swift it may be more or less of a plunge, and after the plunge the water is likely to pause on the third turn, in a natural pool, before resuming its triple action again. And so, in my ravine, some seasons later, I ventured to detain the overflow of my first pool on a second and a third lingering place, augmenting the water supply by new springs developed in the bottoms of the new pools. The second pool has a surface of a thousand square feet, the third spans nineteen hundred, and there are fish in all three, hatched there—"pumpkin-seed" included, but also trout—among spontaneous bulrushes, pond-lilies, flags, and dainty water-weeds; and sometimes at night, when the reflected glory of a ten-o'clock full moon shines up from it to the stone exedra on the lawn, I seem to have taken my Praxitelean curves so directly from Nature that she thinks she took them herself from me and thanks me for the suggestion.

Please observe that of great gardens, or of costly gardens whether great or only costly, we here say nothing. Our theme is such a garden as a householder may himself make and keep or for which, at most, he needs professional advice only in its first planning, and for its upkeep one gardener, with one occasional helper in pressing seasons or in constructional work.

Constructional work. Dams, for example. In two of my dams I built cores of concrete and thus made acquaintance with that interesting material. Later I pressed the acquaintanceship, made garden and grove seats, a table or two, a very modest fountain for a single jet of water in my highest, smallest fish-pool, and even a flight of steps with a pair of gaîne-shaped pedestals—suggested by a sculptor friend—at their top. The exedra I mentioned just now is of concrete. The stuff is a temptation to be wary of. The ordinary gray sort—I have touched no other—is a humble medium, and pretentious designs in humble materials are one of the worst, and oldest, of garden incongruities. In my ventures with concrete I have studied for grace in form but grace subordinated to stability, and have shunned embellishment. Embellishment for its own sake is the easiest and commonest sin against good art wherever art becomes self-conscious. It is having a riotous time just now in concrete. I have rarely seen a commercial concrete garden-seat which was not more ornate than I should want it for my own acre. I happen to have two or three articles in my garden which are a trifle elaborate but they are of terra-cotta, are not home-made and would be plainer could I have found them so.

A garden needs furniture only less than a house, and concrete is a boon to "natural" gardening, being inexpensive, rustic, and imperishable. I fancy a chief reason why there is such inconsiderate dearth of seats and steps in our American amateur gardens is the old fashion—so well got rid of at any cost—of rustic cedar and hickory stairs and benches. "Have none of them," was Colonel Waring's injunction; "they are forever out of repair."

But I fear another reason is that so often our gardens are neither for private ease nor social joy, but for public display and are planned mainly for street exhibition. That is the way we commonly treat garden fountains! We make a smug show of unfenced, unhedged, universal hospitality across a sidewalk boundary which nevertheless we hold inviolate—sometimes by means of a painted sign or gas-pipe—and never say "Have a seat" to the dearest friend in any secluded nook of our shrubberies, if there is such a nook. How many of us know a fountain beside an embowered seat where one,—or two,—with or without the book of verses, can sit and hear it whisper or watch the moonlight cover it with silent kisses? In my limited experience I have known of but two. One is by the once favorite thought-promoting summer seat of Augustus Saint-Gaudens on his own home acre in Vermont; the other I need not particularize further than to say that it is one of the things which interlock and unify a certain garden and grove.

The bringing of the grove out on the lawn and the pushing of the lawn in under the grove was one of the early tasks of my own acre.

When the house was built its lot and others backed up to a hard, straight rear line where the old field had halted at its fence and where the woods began on ground that fell to the river at an angle of from forty to fifty degrees. Here my gifted friend and adviser gave me a precept got from his earlier gifted friend and adviser, Frederick Law Olmsted: that passing from any part of a pleasure-ground to any part next it should be entirely safe and easy or else impossible. By the application of this maxim I brought my lawn and grove together in one of the happiest of marriages. For I proceeded, by filling with earth (and furnace ashes), to carry the lawn in, practically level, beyond the old fence line and under the chestnuts and pines sometimes six feet, sometimes twelve, until the difficult and unsafe forty or fifty degrees of abrupt fall were changed to an impassable sixty and seventy degrees, and every one's instinctive choice of way was the contour paths.

At the same time this has preserved, and even enhanced, the place's wildness, especially the wild flowers and the low-nesting birds. Sometimes a few yards of retaining-wall, never cemented, always laid up dry and with a strong inward batter, had to be put in to avoid smothering the roots of some great tree; for, as everybody knows and nearly everybody forgets, roots, like fishes, must have air. In one place, across the filled head of a ravine, the wall, though but a scant yard high, is fifty feet long, and there is another place where there should be one like it. In this work no tree was sacrificed save one noble oak done to death by a youth who knew but forgot that roots must have air.

Not to make the work expensive it was pursued slowly, through many successive seasons; yet before even its easy, first half was done the lawn was in under the grove on an apparently natural, irregular crest line. Moreover the grove was out on the lawn with an even more natural haphazard bordering line; for another operation had been carried on meantime. Trees, souvenir trees, had from time to time been planted on the lawn by visiting friends. Most of them are set close enough to the grove to become a part of it, standing in a careful irregularity which has already obliterated, without molesting, the tree line of the ancient fence.

Young senators among their seniors, they still have much growth to make before they can enter into their full forest dignity, yet Henry Ward Beecher's elm is nearly two feet through and has a spread of fifty; Max O'Rell's white-ash is a foot in diameter and fifty feet high; Edward Atkinson's is something more, and Felix Adler's hemlock-spruce, the maple of Anthony Hope Hawkins, L. Clark Seelye's English ash, Henry van Dyke's white-ash, Sol Smith Russell's linden, and Hamilton Wright Mabie's horse-chestnut are all about thirty-five feet high and cast a goodly shade. Sir James M. Barrie's elm—his and Sir William Robertson Nicoll's, who planted it with him later than the plantings aforementioned—has, by some virtue in the soil or in its own energies, reached a height of nearly sixty-five feet and a diameter of sixteen inches. Other souvenirs are a horse-chestnut planted by Minnie Maddern Fiske, a ginkgo by Alice Freeman Palmer, a beech by Paul van Dyke, a horse-chestnut by Anna Hempstead Branch, another by Sir Sidney Lee, yet another by Mary E. Burt, a catalpa by Madelaine Wynne, a Colorado blue spruce—fitly placed after much labor of mind—by Sir Moses Ezekiel, and a Kentucky coffee-tree by Gerald Stanley Lee and Jennette Lee, of our own town. Among these should also stand the maple of Sir Arthur Conan Doyle, but it was killed in its second winter by an undetected mouse at its roots. Except Sir Moses, all the knights here named received the accolade after their tree plantings, but I draw no moral.

Would it were practicable to transmit to those who may know these trees in later days the scenes of their setting out and to tell just how the words were said which some of the planters spoke. Mr. Beecher, lover of young trees and young children, straightened up after pressing the soil about the roots with hands as well as feet and said: "I cannot wish you to live as long as this tree, but may your children's children and their children sit under its shade." Said Felix Adler to his hemlock-spruce, "Vivat, crescat, floreat"; and a sentiment much like it was implied in Sol Smith Russell's words to the grove's master as they finished putting in his linden together—for he was just then proposing to play Rip Van Winkle, which Joseph Jefferson had finally decided to produce no more: "Here's to your healt', undt der healt' of all your family; may you lif long undt brosper."

We—the first person singular grows tiresome—we might have now, on our acre, a tree planted by Joseph Jefferson had we thought in time to be provided with a sapling, growing, in a tub. Have your prospective souvenir tree already tubbed and waiting. This idea I got from Andrew Carnegie, with whom I had the honor to plant an oak at Skibo Castle and from whom I, like so many others, have had other things almost as good as ideas. Have your prospective souvenir tree tubbed and the tub sunk in the ground, of course, to its rim. Then the dear friend can plant it at any time that he may chance along between March and December. But let no souvenir tree, however planted, be treated, after planting, as other than a living thing if you would be just to it, to your friend, or to yourself. Cultivate it; coax it on; and it will grow two or three or four times as fast as if left to fight its daily battle for life unaided. And do not forbear to plant trees because they grow so slowly. They need not. They do not. With a little attention they grow so swiftly! Before you know it you are sitting in their shade. Besides Sir Arthur's maple the only souvenir tree we have lost was a tulip-tree planted by my friend of half a lifetime, the late Franklin H. Head.

So much for my grove. I write of it not in self-complacency. My many blunders, some of them yet to be made, are a good insurance against that. I write because of the countless acres as good as mine, in this great, dear America, which might now be giving their owners all the healthful pastime, private solace, or solitary or social delights which this one yields, yet which are only "waste lands" or "holes in the ground" because unavailable for house lots or tillage.

And now as to the single acre by measure, of lawn, shrubs, and plants, close around my house; for the reason that it was and is my school of gardening. There was no garden here—I write this in the midst of it—when I began. Ten steps from where I sit there had been a small Indian mound which some one had carefully excavated. I found stone arrow chips on the spot, and one whole arrow-head. So here no one else's earlier skill was in evidence to point my course or impede it. This was my clean new slate and at that time I had never "done a sum" in gardening and got anything like a right answer.

It is emphatically an amateur garden and a book garden: a garden which to me, as to most of us, would have been impossible in any but these days when the whole art of gardening has been printed in books and no amateur is excusable for trying to garden without reading them, or for saying after having read them that he has planned and worked without professional advice. The books are the professional advice, with few drawbacks and with the great advantage that they are ours truly and do not even have to be "'phoned." I should rather have in my library my Bailey's

"American Cyclopedia of Horticulture," than any two garden periodicals once a month. These, too, I value, but, for me, they are over-apt to carry too much deckload of the advice and gentle vauntings of other amateurs. I have an amateur's abhorrence of amateurs! The Cyclopedia knows, and will always send me to the right books if it cannot thresh a matter out with me itself. Before Bailey my fount of knowledge was Mr. E. J. Canning, late of Smith College Botanic Gardens; a spring still far from dry.

As the books enjoin, I began my book-gardening with a plan on paper; not the elaborate thing one pays for when he can give his garden more money than time, but a light sketch, a mere fundamental suggestion. This came professionally from a landscape-architect, Miss Frances Bullard, of Bridgeport, Connecticut, who had just finished plotting the grounds of my neighbor, the college.

I tell of my own garden for another reason: that it shows, I think, how much can be done with how little, if for the doing you take time instead of money. All things come to the garden that knows how to wait. Mine has acquired at leisure a group of effects which would have cost from ten to twenty times as much if got in a hurry. Garden for ten-year results and get them for next to nothing, and at the same time you may quicken speed whenever your exchequer smiles broadly enough. Of course this argument is chiefly for those who have the time and not the money; for by time we mean play time, time which is money lost if you don't play. The garden that gives the most joy, "Joyous Gard," as Sir Launcelot named his, is not to be bought, like a Circassian slave; it must be brought up, like a daughter. How much of life they can miss who can buy whatever they want whenever they want it!

But I tell first of my own garden also because I believe it summarizes to the eye a number of primary book-rules, authoritative "don'ts," by the observance of which a multitude of amateur gardeners may get better results than it yet shows. Nevertheless, I will hardly do more than note a few exceptions to these ground rules, which may give the rules a more convincing force. First of all, "don't" let any of your planting cut or split your place in two. How many a small house-lot lawn we see split down the middle by a row of ornamental shrubs or fruit-trees which might as easily have been set within a few feet of the property line, whose rigidity, moreover, would have best excused the rigidity of the planted line. But such glaring instances aside, there are many subtler ones quite as unfortunate; "don't" be too sure you are not unwittingly furnishing one.

"Don't" destroy the openness of your sward by dotting it with shrubs or pattern flower-beds. To this rule I doubt if a plausible exception could be contrived. It is so sweeping and so primary that we might well withhold it here were we not seeking to state its artistic reason why. Which is, that such plantings are mere eruptions of individual smartness, without dignity and with no part in any general unity; chirping up like pert children in a company presumably trying to be rational.

On the other hand, I hope my acre, despite all its unconscious or unconfessed mistakes, shows pleasantly that the best openness of a lawn is not to be got between unclothed, right-angled and parallel bounds. The more its verdure-clad borders swing in and out the longer they look, not merely because they are longer but also because they interest and lure the eye. "Where are you going?" says the eye.

"Come and see," says the roaming line.

"Don't" plant in stiff lines except in close relation to architectural or legal bounds. A straight horizontal line Nature scarcely knows save in her rocks and on a vaster scale than we here have to do with. Yet straight lines in gardening are often good and fine if only they are lines of real need. Where, when and in what degree it is good to subordinate utility to beauty or beauty to utility depends on time, place and circumstance, but when in doubt "don't" pinch either to pet the other. Oppression is never good art. Yet "don't" cry war, war, where there is no war. A true beauty and a needed utility may bristle on first collision but they soon make friends. Was it not Ruskin himself who wanted to butt the railway-train off the track and paw up the rails—something like that? But even between them and the landscape there is now an entente cordiale. I have seen the hand of Joseph Pennell make beautiful peace with billboards and telegraph-poles and wires.

The railway points us to the fact that along the ground Nature is as innocent of parallel lines, however bent, as of straight ones, and that in landscape-gardening parallels should be avoided unless they are lines of utility. "Don't" lay parallel lines, either straight or curved, where Nature would not and utility need not. Yet my own acre has taught me a modification of this rule so marked as to be almost an exception. On each side of me next my nearest neighbor I have a turfed alley between a continuous bed of flowering shrubs and plants next the division line, and a similar bed whose meanderings border my lawn. At first I gave these two alleys a sinuous course in correspondence with the windings of the bed bordering the lawn—for they were purely ways of pleasure among the flowers, and a loitering course seemed only reasonable. But sinuous lines proved as disappointing in the alleys as they were satisfying out on the lawn, and by and by I saw that whereas the bendings of the open lawn's borders lured and rewarded the eye, the same curves in the alleys obstructed and baffled it. The show of floral charms was piecemeal, momentary and therefore trivial. "Don't" be trivial!

But a cure was easy. I had to straighten but one side of each alley to restore the eye's freedom of perspective, and nothing more was wanting. The American eye's freedom of perspective is one of our great liberties.

Oh, say, can you see—?

I made this change, of course, on the side nearest the straight, property-division bound, where ran an invisible wire fence. Thus the bed on that side was set between two straight parallels, while the bed on the lawn side remained between waving parallels. This gave the best simplicity with the least artificiality. And thus the two lanes are open to view from end to end, yet each has two deep bays on the side nearest the lawn, bays which remain unseen till one actually reaches them in traversing the lane. In such a bay one should always have, I think, some floral revelation of special charm worthy of the seclusion and the surprise. But this thought is only one of a hundred that tell me my garden is not a finished thing. To its true lover a garden never is.

Another sort of bay, the sort resulting from a swift retreat of a line of shrubberies pursued by the lawn and then swinging round and returning upon the lawn in a counter pursuit, I thought I had learned from books and Miss Bullard and had established on my own acre, until I saw the college gardens of Oxford, England, and the landscape work in Hyde Park, London. On my return thence I made haste to give my own garden's in-and-out curves twice the boldness they had had. And doubling their boldness I doubled their beauty. "Don't" ever let your acre's, or half or quarter acre's, ground lines relax into feebleness or shrink into pettiness. "Don't" ever plan a layout for whose free swing your limits are cramped.

"Don't" ever, if you can help it, says another of my old mistakes to me, let your acre lead your guest to any point which can be departed from only by retracing one's steps. Such necessities involve a lapse—not to say collapse—of interest, which makes for dulness and loss of dignity. Lack what my own acre may, I have it now so that by its alleys, lawns and contour paths in garden and grove we can walk and walk through every part of it without once meeting our own tracks, and that is not all because of the pleasant fact that the walks, where not turfed, are covered with pine-straw, of which each new September drops us a fresh harvest.

A garden, we say, should never compel us to go back the way we came; but in truth a garden should never compel us to do anything. Its don'ts should be laid solely on itself. Those applicable to its master, mistress, or guests should all be impossibilities, not requests. "Private grounds, no crossing"—take that away, please, wherever you can, and plant your margins so that there can be no crossing. Wire nettings hidden by shrubberies from all but the shameless trespasser you will find far more effective, more promotive to beauty and more courteous. "Don't" make your garden a garden of don'ts.

For no garden is quite a garden until it is "Joyous Gard." Let not yours or mine be a garden for display. Then our rhododendrons and like splendors will not be at the front gate, and our grounds be less and less worth seeing the farther into them we go. Nor let yours or mine be a garden of pride. The ways of such a garden are not pleasantness nor its paths peace. And let us not have a garden of tiring care or a user up of precious time. That is not good citizenship. Neither let us have an old-trousers, sun-bonnet, black finger-nails garden—especially if you are a woman. A garden that makes a wife, daughter or sister a dowdy is hardly "Joyous Gard." Neither is one which makes itself a mania to her and an affliction to her family. Let us not even have, you or me, a wonder garden—of arboreal or floral curiosities. Perhaps because I have not travelled enough I have never seen a garden of exotics that was a real garden in any good art sense; in any way, that is, lastingly pleasing to a noble spirit. Let your garden, and let mine, be the garden of joy. For the only way it can be that, on and on, year in, year out, is to be so good in art and so finely human in its purposes that to have it and daily keep it will make us more worth while to ourselves and to mankind than to go without it.

THE AMERICAN GARDEN

Almost any good American will admit it to be a part of our national social scheme, I think,—if we have a social scheme,—that everybody shall aspire to all the refinements of life.

Particularly is it our theory that every one shall propose to give to his home all the joys and graces which are anywhere associated with the name of home. Yet until of late we have neglected the art of gardening. Now and then we see, or more likely we read about, some garden of wonderful beauty; but the very fame of it points the fact that really artistic gardening is not democratically general with us.

Our cities and towns, without number, have the architect and the engineer, for house and for landscape, for sky-scrapers and all manner of public works; we have the nurseryman, the florist; we have parks, shaded boulevards and riverside and lakeside drives. Under private ownership we have a vast multitude of exactly rectilinear lawns, extremely bare or else very badly planted; and we have hundreds of thousands of beautiful dames and girls who "love flowers." But our home gardens, our home gardeners, either professional or amateur, where are they? Our smaller cities by scores and our towns by hundreds are full of home-dwellers each privately puzzled to know why every one of his neighbors' houses, however respectable in architecture, stares at him and after him with a vacant, deaf-mute air of having just landed in this country, without friends.

What ails these dwellings is largely lack of true gardening. They will never look like homes, never look really human and benign, that is, until they are set in a gardening worthy of them. For a garden which alike in its dignity and in its modesty is worthy of the house around which it is set, is the smile of the place.

In the small city of Northampton, Massachusetts, there has been for many years an annual prize competition of amateur flower-gardens. In 1913 there were over a thousand homes, about one-fourth of all the dwellings in the town, in this pretty contest. Not all, not half, these competitors could make a show worthy the name of good gardening, but every one of these households stood pledged to do something during the year for the outdoor improvement of the home, and hundreds of their house lots were florally beautiful. If I seem to hurry into a mention of it here it is partly in the notion that such a recital may be my best credentials as the writer of these pages, and partly in the notion that such a concrete example may possibly have a tendency to help on flower-gardening in the country at large and even to aid us in determining what American flower-gardening had best be.

For the reader's better advantage, however, let me first state one or two general ideas which have given this activity and its picturesque results particular aspects and not others.

I lately heard a lady ask an amateur gardener, "What is the garden's foundation principle?"

There was a certain overgrown pomp in the question's form, but that is how she very modestly asked it, and I will take no liberty with its construction. I thought his reply a good one.

"We have all," he said, "come up from wild nature. In wild nature there are innumerable delights, but they are qualified by countless inconveniences. The cave, tent, cabin, cottage and castle have gradually been evolved by an orderly accumulation and combination of defences and conveniences which secure to us a host of advantages over wild nature and wild man. Yet rightly we are loath to lose any more of nature than we must in order to be her masters and her children in one, and to gather from her the largest fund of profit and delight she can be made to yield. Hence around the cottage, the castle or the palace waves and blooms the garden."

Was he not right? This is why, in our pleasant Northampton affair, we have accepted it as our first rule of private gardening that the house is the climacteric note.

This is why the garden should never be more architectural and artificial than the house of which it is the setting, and this is why the garden should grow less and less architectural and artificial as it draws away from the house. To say the same thing in reverse, the garden, as it approaches the house, should accept more and more discipline—domestication—social refinement, until the house itself at length seems as unabruptly and naturally to grow up out of the garden as the high keynote rises at the end of a lady's song.

By this understanding of the matter what a fine truce-note is blown between the contending advocates of "natural" and of "formal" gardening! The right choice between these two aspects of the art, and the right degree in either choice, depend on the character of the house. The house is a part of the garden. It is the garden's brow and eyes. In gardening, almost the only thing which costs unduly is for us to try to give our house some other house's garden. One's private garden should never be quite so far removed from a state of nature as his house is. Its leading function should be to delight its house's inmates (and intimates) in things of nature so refined as to inspire and satisfy their happiest moods. Therefore no garden should cost, nor look as if it cost, an outlay of money, time or toil that cramps the house's own ability to minister to the genuine bodily needs and spiritual enlargements of its indwellers; and therefore, also, it should never seem to cost, in its first making or in its daily keeping, so much pains as to lack, itself, a garden's supreme essential—tranquillity.

So, then, to those who would incite whole streets of American towns to become florally beautiful, "formal" gardening seems hardly the sort to recommend. About the palatial dwellings of men of princely revenue it may be enchanting. There it appears quite in place. For with all its exquisite artificiality it still is nearer to nature than the stately edifice it surrounds and adorns. But for any less costly homes it costs too much. It is expensive in its first outlay and it demands constantly the greatest care and the highest skill. Our ordinary American life is too busy for it unless the ground is quite handed over to the hired professional and openly betrays itself as that very unsatisfying thing, a "gardener's garden."

Our ordinary American life is also too near nature for the formal garden to come in between. Unless our formal gardening is of some inexpensive sort our modest dwelling-houses give us an anticlimax, and there is no inexpensive sort of formal gardening. Except in the far south our American climate expatriates it.

A very good practical rule would be for none of us to venture upon such gardening until he is well able to keep up an adequate greenhouse. A formal garden without a greenhouse or two—or three—is a glorious army on a war footing, but without a base of supplies. It is largely his greenhouses which make the public gardener and the commercial florist so misleading an example for the cottager to follow in his private gardening.

To be beautiful, formal gardening requires stately proportions. Without these it is almost certain to be petty and frivolous. In the tiny gardens of British and European peasants, it is true, a certain formality of design is often practised with pleasing success; but these gardens are a by-product of peasant toil, and in America we have no joy in contemplating an American home limited to the aspirations of peasant life. In such gardening there is a constraint, a lack of natural freedom, a distance from nature, and a certain contented subserviency, which makes it—however fortunate it may be under other social conditions—wholly unfit to express the buoyant, not to say exuberant, complacencies of the American home. For these we want, what we have not yet quite evolved, the American garden. When this comes it must come, of course, unconsciously; but we may be sure it will not be much like the gardens of any politically shut-in people. No, not even of those supreme artists in gardening, the Japanese. It will express the traits of our American domestic life; our strong individuality and self-assurance, our sense of unguarded security, our affability and unexclusiveness and our dislike to high-walled privacy. If we would hasten its day we must make way for it along the lines of these traits.

On the other hand, if in following these lines we can contrive to adhere faithfully to the worldwide laws of all true art, who knows but our very gardening may tend to correct more than one shortcoming or excess in our national character?

In our Northampton experiment it has been our conviction from the beginning that for a private garden to be what it should be—to have a happy individuality—a countenance of its own—one worthy to be its own—it must in some practical way be the fruit of its householder's own spirit and not merely of some hired gardener's. If one can employ a landscape-architect, all very well; but the most of us cannot, and after all, the true landscape-architect, the artist gardener, works on this principle and seeks to convey into every garden distinctively the soul of the household for which it springs and flowers.

"Since when it grows and smells, I swear,
Not of itself but thee."

Few American householders, however, have any enthusiasm for this theory, which many would call high-strung, and as we in Northampton cannot undertake to counsel and direct our neighbors' hired helps, we enroll in the main branch of our competition only those who garden for themselves and hire no labor. To such the twenty-one prizes, ranging from two dollars and a half up to fifteen dollars, are a strong incentive, and by such the advice of visiting committees is eagerly sought and followed. The public educative value of the movement is probably largest under these limitations, for in this way we show what beautiful results may be got on smallest grounds and with the least outlay. Its private educative value, too, is probably largest thus, because thus we disseminate as a home delight a practical knowledge of æsthetic principles among those who may at any time find it expedient to become wage-earning gardeners on the home grounds of the well-to-do.

The competing gardens being kept wholly without hired labor, of course our constant advice to all contestants is to shun formal gardening. It is a pity that in nearly all our cities and towns the most notable examples of gardening are found in the parks, boulevards, and cemeteries. By these flaring displays thousands of modest cottagers who might easily provide, on their small scale, lovely gardens about their dwellings at virtually no cost and with no burdensome care, get a notion that this, and this only, is artistic gardening and hence that a home garden for oneself would be too expensive and troublesome to be thought of. On the other hand, a few are tempted to mimic them on a petty scale, and so spoil their little grass-plots and amuse, without entertaining, their not more tasteful but only less aspiring neighbors. In Northampton, in our Carnegie prize contest—so called for a very sufficient and pleasant reason—our counsel is to avoid all mimicry in gardening as we would avoid it in speech or in gait. Sometimes we do not mind being repetitious. "In gardening" we say—as if we had never said it before—"almost the only thing which costs unduly—in money or in mortification—is for one to try to give himself somebody else's garden!" Often we say this twice to the same person.

One of the reasons we give against it is that it leads to toy gardening, and toy gardening is of all sorts the most pitiful and ridiculous. "No true art," we say, "can tolerate any make-believe which is not in some way finer than the reality it simulates. In other words, imitation should always be in the nature of an amiable condescension. Whatever falseness, pretension or even mere frailty or smallness, suggests to the eye the ineffectuality of a toy is out of place in any sort of gardening." We do not actually speak all this, but we imply it, and we often find that the mere utterance of the one word, "toy gardening," has a magical effect to suggest all the rest and to overwhelm with contrition the bad taste and frivolity of many a misguided attempt at adornment. At that word of exorcism joints of cerulean sewer-pipe crested with scarlet geraniums, rows of whited cobbles along the walk or drive like a cannibal's skulls around his hut, purple paint-kegs of petunias on the scanty doorsteps, crimson wash-kettles of verbenas, ant-hill rockeries, and wellsweeps and curbs where no wells are, steal modestly and forever into oblivion.

Now, when we so preach we try also to make it very plain that there is not one set of rules for gardening on a small scale of expense in a small piece of ground, and another set for gardening on a larger scale. For of course the very thing which makes the small garden different from the large, the rich man's from the poor man's, the Scotch or Italian peasant's from the American mechanic's, or the public garden from the private, is the universal and immutable oneness of the great canons of art. One of our competitors, having honestly purged her soul of every impulse she may ever have had to mimic the gardening of the cemeteries, planted her dooryard with a trueness of art which made it the joy of all beholders. Only then was it that a passing admirer stopped and cried: "Upon me soul, Mrs. Anonyma, yir gyairden looks joost loike a pooblic pairk!" He meant—without knowing it—that the spot was lovely for not trying to look the least bit like a public park, and he was right. She had kept what it would be well for the public gardeners to keep much better than some of them do—the Moral Law of Gardening.

There is a moral law of gardening. No garden should ever tell a lie.

No garden should ever put on any false pretence. No garden should ever break a promise. To the present reader these proclamations may seem very trite; it may seem very trite to say that if anything in or of a garden is meant for adornment, it must adorn; but we have to say such things to many who do not know what trite means—who think it is something you buy from the butcher. A thing meant for adornment, we tell them, must so truly and sufficiently adorn as to be worth all the room and attention it takes up. Thou shalt not let anything in thy garden take away thy guest's attention without repaying him for it; it is stealing.

A lady, not in our competition but one of its most valued patronesses, lately proposed to herself to place in the centre of a wide, oval lawn a sun-dial and to have four paths cross the grass and meet there. But on reflection the query came to her—

"In my unformal garden of simplest grove and sward will a sun-dial—posing in an office it never performed there, and will never again be needed for anywhere—a cabinet relic now—will a posed sun-dial be interesting enough when it is arrived at to justify a special journey and four kept-up paths which cut my beautiful grass-plot into quarters?"

With that she changed her mind—a thing the good gardener must often do—and appointed the dial to a place where one comes upon it quite incidentally while moving from one main feature of the grounds to another. It is now a pleasing, mild surprise instead of a tame fulfilment of a showy promise; pleasing, after all, it must, however, be admitted, to the toy-loving spirit, since the sun-dial has long been, and henceforth ever will be, an utterly useless thing in a garden, only true to art when it stands in an old garden, a genuine historical survival of its day of true utility. Only in such a case does the sun-dial belong to the good morals of gardening. But maybe this is an overstrict rule for the majority of us who are much too fond of embellishments and display—the rouge and powder of high art.

On the other hand, we go to quite as much pains to say that though a garden may not lie nor steal, it may have its concealments; they are as right as they are valuable. One of the first steps in the making of a garden should be to determine what to hide and how most gracefully to hide it. A garden is a house's garments, its fig-leaves, as we may say, and the garden's concealments, like its revelations, ought always to be in the interest of comfort, dignity, and charm.

We once had a very bumptious member on our board of judges. "My dear madam!" he exclaimed to an aspirant for the prizes, the underpinning of whose dwelling stood out unconcealed by any sprig of floral growth, "your house is barefooted! Nobody wants to see your house's underpinning, any more than he wants to see your own!"

It is not good to be so brusque about non-penitentiary offences, but skilful and lovely concealments in gardening were his hobby. To another he whispered, "My dear sir, tell your pretty house her petticoat shows!" and to yet another, "Take all those shrubs out of the middle of your lawn and 'plant out' with them every feature of your house which would be of no interest to you if the house were not yours. Your house's morals may be all right, but its manners are insufferable, it talks so much about itself and its family." To a fourth he said: "In a gardening sense your house makes too much noise; you can hear its right angles hit the ground. Muffle them! Muffle your architectural angles in foliage and bloom. Up in the air they may be ever so correct and fine, but down in the garden and unclothed they are heinous, heinous!"

Another precept we try to inculcate in our rounds among the gardens, another commandment in the moral law of gardening, is that with all a garden's worthy concealments it should never, and need never, be frivolous or be lacking in candor. I know an amateur gardener—and the amateur gardener, like the amateur photographer, sometimes ranks higher than the professional—who is at this moment altering the location of a sidewalk gate which by an earlier owner was architecturally misplaced for the sole purpose of making a path with curves—and such curves!—instead of a straight and honest one, from the street to the kitchen. When a path is sent on a plain business errand it should never loaf. And yet those lines of a garden's layout which are designed not for business but for pleasure, should never behave as though they were on business; they should loiter just enough to make their guests feel at ease, while not enough to waste time. How like a perfect lady, or a perfect gentleman, is—however humble or exalted its rank—a garden with courtly manners!

As to manners, our incipient American garden has already developed one trait which distinguishes it from those beyond the Atlantic. It is a habit which reminds one of what somebody has lately said about Americans themselves: that, whoever they are and whatever their manners may be, they have this to their credit, that they unfailingly desire and propose to be polite. The thing we are hinting at is our American gardens' excessive openness. Our people have, or until just now had, almost abolished the fence and the hedge. A gard, yard, garth, garden, used to mean an enclosure, a close, and implied a privacy to its owner superior to any he enjoyed outside of it. But now that we no longer have any military need of privacy we are tempted—are we not?—to overlook its spiritual value. We seem to enjoy publicity better. In our American eagerness to publish everything for everybody and to everybody, we have published our gardens—published them in paper bindings; that is to say, with their boundaries visible only on maps filed with the Registrar of Deeds.

Foreigners who travel among us complain that we so overdo our good-natured endurance of every public inconvenience that we have made it a national misfortune and are losing our sense of our public rights. This obliteration of private boundaries is an instance. Our public spirit and out imperturbability are flattered by it, but our gardens, except among the rich, have become American by ceasing to be gardens.

I have a neighbor who every year plants a garden of annuals. He has no fence, but two of his neighbors have each a setter dog. These dogs are rarely confined. One morning I saw him put in the seed of his lovely annuals and leave his smoothly raked beds already a pleasant show and a prophecy of delight while yet without a spray of green. An hour later I saw those two setter dogs wrestling and sprawling around in joyous circles all over those garden beds. "Gay, guiltless pair!" What is one to do in such a case, in a land where everybody is expected to take everything good-naturedly, and where a fence is sign of a sour temper? Of course he can do as others do, and have no garden. But to have no garden is a distinct poverty in a householder's life, whether he knows it or not, and—suppose he very much wants a garden?

They were the well-to-do who began this abolition movement against enclosures and I have an idea it never would have had a beginning had there prevailed generally, democratically, among us a sentiment for real gardening, and a knowledge of its practical principles; for with this sentiment and knowledge we should have had that sweet experience of outdoor privacy for lack of which we lose one of the noblest charms of home. The well-to-do started the fashion, it cost less money to follow than to withstand it and presently the landlords of the poor utilized it.

The poor man—the poor woman—needs the protection of a fence to a degree of which the well-to-do know nothing. In the common interest of the whole community, of any community, the poor man—the poor woman—ought to have a garden; but if they are going to have a garden they ought to have a fence. We in Northampton know scores of poor homes whose tenants strive year after year to establish some floral beauty about them, and fail for want of enclosures. The neighbors' children, their dogs, their cats, geese, ducks, hens—it is useless. Many refuse to make the effort; some, I say, make it and give it up, and now and then some one wins a surprising and delightful success. Two or three such have taken high prizes in our competition. The two chief things which made their triumph possible were, first, an invincible passion for gardening, and, second, poultry-netting.

A great new boon to the home gardener they are, these wire fencings and nettings. With them ever so many things may be done now at a quarter or tenth of what they would once have cost. Our old-fashioned fences were sometimes very expensive, sometimes very perishable, sometimes both. Also they were apt to be very ugly. Yet instead of concealing them we made them a display, while the shrubbery which should have masked them in leaf and bloom stood scattered over the lawn, each little new bush by itself, visibly if not audibly saying—

"You'd scarce expect one of my age——"

etc.; the shrubs orphaned, the lawn destroyed.

If the enclosure was a hedge it had to be a tight one or else it did not enclose. Now wire netting charms away these embarrassments. Your hedge can be as loose as you care to have it, while your enclosure may be rigidly effective yet be hidden from the eye by undulating fence-rows; and as we now have definite bounds and corners to plant out, we do not so often as formerly need to be reminded of Frederick Law Olmsted's favorite maxim, "Take care of the corners, and the centres will take care of themselves."

Here there is a word to be added in the interest of home-lovers, whose tastes we properly expect to find more highly trained than those of the average tenant cottager. Our American love of spaciousness leads us to fancy that—not to-day or to-morrow, but somewhere in a near future—we are going to unite our unfenced lawns in a concerted park treatment: a sort of wee horticultural United States comprised within a few city squares; but ever our American individualism stands broadly in the way, and our gardens almost never relate themselves to one another with that intimacy which their absence of boundaries demands in order to take on any special beauty, nobility, delightsomeness, of gardening. The true gardener—who, if he is reading this, must be getting very tired of our insistent triteness—carefully keeps in mind the laws of linear and of aërial perspective, no matter how large or small the garden. The relative stature of things, both actual and prospective; their breadth; the breadth or slenderness, darkness or lightness, openness or density, of their foliage; the splendor or delicacy of their flowers, whether in size or in color; the season of their blooming; the contour of the grounds—all these points must be taken into account in determining where things are to stand and how be grouped. Once the fence or hedge was the frame of the picture; but now our pictures, on almost any street of unpalatial, comfortable homes, touch edge to edge without frames, and the reason they do not mar one another's effects is that they have no particular effects to be marred, but lie side by side as undiscordantly as so many string instruments without strings. Let us hope for a time when they will rise in insurrection, resolved to be either parts of a private park, or each one a whole private garden.

In our Carnegie prize contest nothing yields its judges more pleasure than to inculcate the garden rules of perspective to which we have just referred and to see the blissful complacency of those who successfully carry them out. I have now in my mind's eye a garden to which was awarded the capital prize of 1903. A cottage of maybe six small rooms crowns a high bank on a corner where two rural streets cross. There are a few square yards of lawn on its front, and still fewer (scarcely eight or ten) on the side next the cross-street, but on the other two sides there is nearly a quarter of an acre. On these two sides the limits touch other gardens, and all four sides are entirely without fencing. From the front sward have been taken away a number of good shrubs which once broke it into ineffectual bits, and these have been grouped against the inward and outward angles of the house. The front porch is garlanded—not smothered—with vines whose flowers are all white, pink, blue or light purple. About the base of the porch and of all the house's front, bloom flowers of these same delicate tints, the tallest nearest the house, the lesser at their knees and feet. The edges of the beds—gentle waves that never degenerate to straightness—are thickly bordered with mignonette. Not an audacious thing, not a red blossom nor a strong yellow one, nor one broad leaf, nor any mass of dense or dark foliage, comes into view until one reaches a side of the dwelling. But there at once he finds the second phase in a crescendo of floral colors. The base of the house, and especially those empty eye-sockets, the cellar windows, are veiled in exultant bloom, yellows predominating. Then at the back of the place comes the full chorus, and red flowers overmaster the yellow, though the delicate tints with which the scheme began are still present to preserve the dignity and suavity of all—the ladies of the feast. The paths are only one or two and they never turn abruptly and ask you to keep off their corners; they have none. Neither have the flower-beds. They flow wideningly around the hard turnings of the house with the grace of a rivulet. Out on the two wider sides of the lawn nothing breaks the smooth green but a well-situated tree or two until the limits of the premises are reached, and there, in lines that widen and narrow and widen again and hide the surveyor's angles, the flowers rise once more in a final burst of innumerable blossoms and splendid hues—a kind of sunset of the garden's own.

When this place, five seasons ago, first entered the competition, it could hardly be called a garden at all. Yet it was already superior to many rivals. In those days it seemed to us as though scarcely one of our working people in a hundred knew that a garden was anything more than a bed of flowers set down anywhere and anyhow. It was a common experience for us to be led by an unkept path and through a patch of weeds or across an ungrassed dooryard full of rubbish, in order to reach a so-called garden which had never spoken a civil word to the house nor got one from it. Now, the understanding is that every part of the premises, every outdoor thing on the premises—path, fence, truck-patch, stable, stable-yard, hen-yard, tennis or croquet-court—everything is either a part of the garden or is so reasonably related to it that from whatever point one views the place he beholds a single satisfactory picture.

This, I say, is the understanding. I do not say that even among our prize-winners anybody has yet perfectly attained this, although a few have come very near it. With these the main surviving drawback is that the artistic effect is each season so long coming and passes away so soon—cometh up as a flower and presently has withered.

One of our most gifted literary critics a while ago pointed out the poetic charm of evanescence; pointed it out more plainly, I fancy, than it has ever been shown before. But evanescence has this poetic charm chiefly in nature, almost never in art. The transitoriness of a sunset glory, or of human life, is rife with poetic pathos because it is a transitoriness which cannot be helped. Therein lay the charm of that poetic wonder and marvel of its day (1893) the Columbian Exposition's "White City"; it was an architectural triumph and glory which we could not have except on condition that it should vanish with the swiftness of an aurora. Even so, there would have been little poetry in its evanescence if, through bad workmanship or any obvious folly, it had failed to fulfil the transient purpose for which it was erected. The only poetic evanescence is the evanescence that is inevitable. An unnecessary evanescence in things we make is bad art. If I remember the story correctly, it was to a Roman lady that Benvenuto Cellini took the exquisite waxen model of some piece of goldsmithing she had commissioned him to execute for her. So delighted was she with this mere model that she longed to keep it and called it the perfection of art, or some such word. But Benvenuto said, No, he could not claim for it the high name of art until he should have reproduced it in gold, that being the most worthy material in which it would endure the use for which it was designed.

Unless the great Italian was in error, then, a garden ought not to be so largely made up of plants which perish with the summer as to be, at their death, no longer a garden. Said that harsh-spoken judge whom we have already once or twice quoted—that shepherd's-dog of a judge—at one of the annual bestowals of our Carnegie garden prizes:

"Almost any planting about the base of a building, fence or wall is better than none; but for this purpose shrubs are far better than annual flowers. Annuals do not sufficiently mask the hard, offensive right-angles of the structure's corners or of the line whence it starts up from the ground. And even if sometimes they do, they take so long to grow enough to do it, and are so soon gone with the first cold blast, that the things they are to hide are for the most of the year not hidden. Besides which, even at their best moments, when undoubtedly they are very beautiful, they have not a sufficiently substantial look to be good company for the solid structure they are set against. Sweetly, modestly, yet obstinately, they confess to every passer-by that they did not come, but were put there and were put there only last spring. Shrubs, contrariwise, give a feeling that they have sprung and grown there in the course of nature and of the years, and so convey to the house what so many American homes stand in want of—a quiet air of being long married and a mother of growing children.

"Flowering shrubs of well-chosen kinds are in leaf two-thirds of the year, and their leafless branches and twigs are a pleasing relief to the structure's cold nakedness even through the winter. I have seen a house, whose mistress was too exclusively fond of annuals, stand waiting for its shoes and stockings from October clear round to August, and then barefooted again in October. In such gardening there is too much of love's labor lost. If one's grounds are so small that there is no better place for the annuals they can be planted against the shrubs, as the shrubs are planted against the building or fence. At any rate they should never be bedded out in the midst of the lawn, and quite as emphatically they should never, alone, be set to mark the boundary lines of a property."

It is hoped these sayings, quoted or otherwise, may seem the more in place here because they contemplate the aspects likely to characterize the American garden whenever that garden fully arrives. We like largeness. There are many other qualities to desire, and to desire even more; but if we give them also the liking we truly owe them it is right for us to like largeness. Certainly it is better to like largeness even for itself, rather than smallness for itself. Especially is it right that we should like our gardens to look as large as we can make them appear. Our countless lawns, naked clear up into their rigid corners and to their dividing lines, are naked in revolt against the earlier fashion of spotting them over with shrubs, the easiest as well as the worst way of making a place look small. But a naked lawn does not make the premises look as large, nor does it look as large itself, as it will if planted in the manner we venture to commend to our Northampton prize-seekers. Between any two points a line of shrubbery swinging in and out in strong, graceful undulations appears much longer than a straight one, because it is longer. But, over and above this, it makes the distance between the two points seem greater. Everybody knows the old boast of the landscape-architects—that they can make one piece of ground look twice as large as another of the same measure, however small, by merely grading and planting the two on contrary schemes. The present writer knows one small street in his town, a street of fair dwellings, on which every lawn is diminished to the eye by faulty grading.

For this he has no occasion to make himself responsible but there are certain empty lots not far from him for whose aspect he is answerable, having graded them himself (before he knew how). He has repeatedly heard their depth estimated at ninety feet, never at more. In fact it is one hundred and thirty-nine. However, he has somewhat to do also with a garden whose grading was quite as bad—identical, indeed—whose fault has been covered up and its depth made to seem actually greater than it is, entirely by a corrective planting of its shrubbery.

One of the happiest things about gardening is that when it is bad you can always—you and time—you and year after next—make it good. It is very easy to think of the plants, beds and paths of a garden as things which, being once placed, must stay where they are; but it is shortsighted and it is fatal to effective gardening. We should look upon the arrangement of things in our garden very much as a housekeeper looks on the arrangement of the furniture in her house. Except buildings, pavements and great trees—and not always excepting the trees—we should regard nothing in it as permanent architecture but only as furnishment and decoration. At favorable moments you will make whatever rearrangement may seem to you good. A shrub's mere being in a certain place is no final reason that it should stay there; a shrub or a dozen shrubs—next spring or fall you may transplant them. A shrub, or even a tree, may belong where it is this season, and the next and the next; and yet in the fourth year, because of its excessive growth, of the more desired growth of something else, or of some rearrangement of other things, that spot may be no longer the best place for it.

Very few shrubs are injured by careful and seasonable, even though repeated, transplanting. Many are benefited by one or another effect of the process: by the root pruning they get, by the "division," by the change of soil, by change of exposure or even by backset in growth. Transplanting is part of a garden's good discipline. It is almost as necessary to the best results as pruning—on which grave subject there is no room to speak here. The owner even of an American garden should rule his garden, not be ruled by it. Yet he should rule without oppression, and it will not be truly American if it fails to show at a glance that it is not overgardened.

Thus do we propose to exhort our next season's competitors as this fall and winter they gather at our projected indoor garden-talks, or as we go among them to offer counsel concerning their grounds plans for next spring. And we hope not to omit to say, as we had almost omitted to say here, in behalf of the kind of garden we preach, that shrubs, the most of them, require no great enrichment of the soil—an important consideration. And we shall take much care to recommend the perusal of books on gardening. Once this gentle art was largely kept a close secret of craftsmen; but now all that can be put into books is in books, and the books are non-technical, brief and inexpensive; or if voluminous and costly, as some of the best needs must be, are in the public libraries. In their pages are a host of facts (indexed!) which once had to be burdensomely remembered. For one preoccupied with other cares—as every amateur gardener ought to be—these books are no mean part of his equipment; they are as necessary to his best gardening as the dictionary to his best English.

What a daily, hourly, unfailing wonder are the modern opportunities and facilities by which we are surrounded! If the present reader and the present writer, and maybe a few others, will but respond to them worthily, who knows but we may ourselves live to see, and to see as democratically common as telephones and electric cars, the American garden? Of course there is ever and ever so much more to be said about it, and the present writer is not at all weary; but he hears his reader's clock telling the hour and feels very sure it is correct.

WHERE TO PLANT WHAT

Often one's hands are too heavily veneered with garden loam for him to go to his books to verify a quotation. It was the great Jefferson, was it not, who laid into the foundations of American democracy the imperishable maxim that "That gardening is best which gardens the least"? My rendition of it may be more a parody than a quotation but, whatever its inaccuracy, to me it still sounds Jeffersonian—Joseph Jeffersonian.

Whether we read it "garden" or "govern," it has this fine mark of a masterful utterance, that it makes no perceptible effort to protect itself against the caviller or the simpleton; from men, for instance, who would interpret it as meaning that the only perfect government, or gardening, is none at all. Speaking from the point of view of a garden-lover, I suppose the true signification is that the best government is the government which procures and preserves the noblest happiness of the community with the least enthralment of the individual.

Now, I hope that as world-citizens and even as Americans we may bear in mind that, while this maxim may be wholly true, it is not therefore the whole truth. What maxim is? Let us ever keep a sweet, self-respecting modesty with which to confront and consort with those who see the science of government, or art of gardening, from the standpoint of some other equally true fraction of the whole truth. All we need here maintain for our Jeffersonian maxim is that its wide domination in American sentiment explains the larger part of all the merits and faults of American government—and American gardening. It accounts for nearly all our American laws and ordinances, manners, customs, and whims, and in the great discussion of Where to Plant What (in America) no one need hope to prevail who does not recognize that this high principle of American democracy is the best rule for American gardening. That gardening is best, for most Americans, which best ministers to man's felicity with least disturbance of nature's freedom.

Hence the initial question—a question which every amateur gardener must answer for himself. How much subserviency of nature to art and utility is really necessary to my own and my friends' and neighbors' best delight? For—be not deceived—however enraptured of wild nature you may be, you do and must require of her some subserviency close about your own dwelling. You cannot there persistently enjoy the wolf and the panther, the muskrat, buzzard, gopher, rattlesnake, poison-ivy and skunk in full swing, as it were. How much, then, of nature's subserviency does the range of your tastes demand? Also, how much will your purse allow? For it is as true in gardening as in statecraft that, your government being once genuinely established, the more of it you have, the more you must pay for it. In gardening, as in government, the cost of the scheme is not in proportion to the goodness or badness of its art, but to its intensity.

This is why the general and very sane inclination of our American preferences is away from that intense sort of gardening called "formal," and toward that rather unfairly termed "informal" method which here, at least, I should like to distinguish as "free-line" gardening. A free people who govern leniently will garden leniently. Their gardening will not be a vexing tax upon themselves, upon others, or upon the garden. Whatever freedom it takes away from themselves or others or the garden will be no more than is required for the noblest delight; and whatever freedom remains untaken, such gardening will help everybody to exercise and enjoy.

The garden of free lines, provided only it be a real garden under a real government, is, to my eye, an angel's protest against every species and degree of tyranny and oppression, and such a garden, however small or extensive, will contain a large proportion of flowering shrubbery. Because a garden should not, any more than my lady's face, have all its features—nose, eyes, ears, lips—of one size? No, that is true of all gardening alike; but because with flowering shrubbery our gardening can be more lenient than with annuals alone, or with only herbaceous plants and evergreens.

So, then, our problem, Where to Plant What, may become for a moment, Where to Plant Shrubbery; and the response of the free-line garden will be, of course, "Remember, concerning each separate shrub, that he or she—or it, if you really prefer the neuter—is your guest, and plant him or her or it where it will best enjoy itself, while promoting the whole company's joy." Before it has arrived in the garden, therefore, learn—and carefully consider—its likes and dislikes, habits, manners and accomplishments and its friendly or possibly unfriendly relations with your other guests. This done, determine between whom and whom you will seat it; between what and what you will plant it, that is, so as to "draw it out," as we say of diffident or reticent persons; or to use it for drawing out others of less social address. But how many a lovely shrub has arrived where it was urgently invited, and found that its host or hostess, or both, had actually forgotten its name! Did not know how to introduce it to any fellow guest, or whether it loved sun or shade, loam, peat, clay, leaf-mould or sand, wetness or dryness; and yet should have found all that out in the proper blue-book (horticultural dictionary) before inviting the poor mortified guest at all.

"Oh, pray be seated—anywhere. Plant yourself alone in the middle. This is Liberty Garden."

"It is no such thing," says the tear-bedewed beauty to herself; "it's Anarchy Garden." Yet, like the lady she is, she stays where she is put, and gets along surprisingly well.

New England calls Northampton one of her most beautiful towns. But its beauty lies in the natural landscape in and around it, in the rise, fall, and swing of the seat on which it sits, the graceful curving of its streets, the noble spread of its great elms and maples, the green and blue openness of grounds everywhere about its modest homes and its highly picturesque outlook upon distant hills and mountains and intervening meadows and fields, with the Connecticut winding through. Its architecture is in three or four instances admirable though not extraordinary, and, as in almost every town in our vast America, there are hardly five householders in it who are really skilled flower-gardeners, either professional or amateur.

As the present century was coming in, however, the opportunity, through private flower-gardening, to double or quadruple the town's beauty and to do it without great trouble or expense, yet with great individual delight and social pleasure, came to the lively notice of a number of us. It is, then, for the promotion of this object throughout all our bounds, and not for the perfection of the art for its own sake, that we maintain this competition and award these "Carnegie" prizes. Hence certain features of our method the value and necessity of which might not be clear to the casual inquirer without this explanation.

May I repeat it? Not to reward two or three persons yearly for reaching some dizzy peak of art unattainable by ordinary taste and skill, nor to reward one part of the town or one element of its people for gardening better than another, nor to promote the production of individual plants or flowers of extraordinary splendor, nor even to incite children to raise patches of flowers, is our design; but to make the modest and democratic art of Where to Plant What (an art, nevertheless, quite beyond the grasp of children) so well known and so valued that its practical adoption shall overrun the whole town.

To this end we have divided our field into seven districts, in each of which the number of gardens is about the same. In each of these seven districts only three prizes (out of twenty-one) may be taken in any one season. Consequently three prizes must fall to each district every year. Yet the best garden of all still carries off the capital prize, the second-best may win the second, and cannot take a lower than the third, and the lowest awards go into the district showing the poorest results. Even this plan is so modified as further to stimulate those who strive against odds of location or conditions, for no district is allowed to receive two prizes consecutive in the list. The second prize cannot be bestowed in the same district in which the first is being awarded, though the third can. The third cannot go into the same district as the second, though the fourth may. And so on to the twenty-first. Moreover, a garden showing much improvement over the previous season may take a prize, as against a better garden which shows no such improvement. Also no garden can take the capital prize twice nor ever take a prize not higher than it has taken before. The twenty-one prizes are for those who hire no help in their gardening; two others are for those who reserve the liberty to employ help, and still another two are exclusively for previous winners of the capital prize, competing among themselves. In each of the five districts a committee of ladies visits the competing gardens, inspecting, advising, encouraging, sometimes learning more than they teach, and reporting to headquarters, the People's Institute. At these headquarters, on two acres of ground in the heart of the city, we have brought gradually into shape, on a plan furnished by Frederick Law Olmsted's Sons, Landscape Architects, of Boston (Brookline), a remarkably handsome garden of flowers and shrubbery designed as a model for the guidance of those in the competition who seek to combine artistic beauty with inexpensiveness. From time to time we have given at these headquarters winter courses of lectures on practical flower-gardening.

As a result we have improved, and are still improving, the aspect of entire streets and are interesting the whole city.

But to return to our discussion. Here is a short story of two ladies. They are not in our competition, though among its most ardent well-wishers. A friend had given one of them a bit of green, woody growth some two feet high and half an inch thick. She had a wee square bit of front grass-plot something larger than a table-cloth, but certainly not large enough for a game of marbles. In the centre of this bit of grass she planted her friend's gift. Then came our other lady, making a call, and with her best smile of humorous commendation, saying:

"My dear, you have violated the first rule of gardening. You've planted your bush where you wanted it."

The delighted gardener went in the strength of that witticism for forty weeks or at least until some fiend of candor, a brother, like as not, said:

"Yes, truly you have violated the first rule of gardening, for you have put your willow-tree—that's what it is—where a minute's real reflection would have told you you'd wish you hadn't."

Where to Plant What! Plant it where you—and your friends—your friends of best gardening taste—will be glad you planted it when all your things are planted. Please those who know best, and so best please yourself. Nevertheless, beware! Watch yourself! Do so specially when you think you have mastered the whole art. Watch even those who indisputably know better than you do, for everybody makes mistakes which he never would have dreamed he could make. Only the other day I heard an amateur say to a distinguished professional gardener:

"Did you plant those shrubs of gorgeous flower and broad, dark leaf out on your street front purely as a matter of artistic taste?"

"I did," he replied. "I wanted to put my best foot foremost. Wouldn't you?"

"Why should I?" asked the amateur. "I wouldn't begin a song with my highest note, nor a game with my strongest card, nor an address with my most impassioned declaration, nor a sonnet with its most pregnant line. If I should, where were my climax?"

Certainly the amateur had the best of it. A garden is a discourse. A garden is a play. See with what care both the dramatist and the stage-manager avoid putting the best foot foremost. See how warily they hold back the supreme strength of the four or five act piece for the last act but one. There is a charmingly instructive analogy between a garden and a drama. In each you have preparation, progress, climax, and close. And then, also, in each you must have your lesser climaxes leading masterfully up to the supreme one, and a final quiet one to let gratefully down from the giddy height.

In Northampton nearly all of our hundreds of gardens contesting for prizes are plays of only one or two acts. I mean they have only one or two buildings to garden up to and between and around and away from. Yet it is among these one-act plays, these one-house gardens, that I find the art truth most gracefully emphasized, that the best foot should not go foremost. In a large garden a false start may be atoned for by better art farther on and in; but in a small garden, for mere want of room and the chance to forget, a bad start spoils all. No, be the garden a prince's or a cottager's, the climaxes to be got by superiority of stature, by darkness and breadth of foliage and by splendor of bloom belong at its far end. Even in the one-house garden I should like to see the climaxes plural to the extent of two; one immediately at the back of the house, the other at the extreme rear of the ground. At the far end of the lot I would have the final storm of passion and riot of disclosure, and then close about the rear of the house there should be the things of supreme richness, exquisiteness and rarity.

This soft-voiced echo answering back out of the inmost heart of the whole demesne gives genuineness of sentiment to the entire scheme. To plant a conflagration of color against the back fence and stop there would be worse than melodramatic. It would be to close the play with a bang, and even a worthy one-act play does not close with a bang. The back of the lot is not the absolute end of the garden-play. Like the stage-play, the garden-play brings its beholder back at the very last, by a sweet reversion, to the point from which it started. The true garden-lover gardens not mainly for the passer-by, but rather for himself and the friends who come to see him. Even when he treads his garden paths alone he is a pleased and welcome visitor to himself, and shows his garden to himself as to a visitor. Hence there is always at last a turning back to the house or to the front entrance, and this is the play's final lines, the last grouping of the players, the relief of all tension and the descent of the curtain.

One point farther in this direction and we may give our hard-worked analogy a respite. It is this: as those who make and present a play take great pains that, by flashes of revelation to eye and to ear, the secrets most unguessed by the characters in the piece shall be early revealed to the audience and persistently pressed upon its attention, so should the planting of a garden be; that, as if quite without the gardener's or the garden's knowledge, always, to the eye, nostril or ear, some clear disclosure of charm still remote may beckon and lure across easy and tempting distances from nook to nook of the small garden, or from alley to alley and from glade to glade of the large one. Where to Plant What? Plant it as far away as, according to the force of its character or the splendor of its charms, it can stand and beckon back with best advantage for the whole garden.

Thus we generalize. And as long as one may generalize he is

comparatively safe from humiliating criticism. It is only when he begins to name things by name and say what is best for just where, that he touches the naked eyeball (or the funny-bone) of others whose crotchets are not identical with his. Yet in Northampton this is what we have to do, and since the competitors for our prizes always have the Where before they are moved to get and place the What, we find our where-and-what problem easiest to handle when we lift it, so to speak, by the tail. Then it is "What to Plant Where," and for answer we have made a short list of familiar flowering shrubs best suited to our immediate geographical locality. We name only fourteen and we so describe each as to indicate clearly enough, without dictating, whereabouts to put it. We begin:

"Azalea. Our common wild azalea is the flowering bush best known as 'swamp honeysuckle.' The two azaleas listed here, A. mollis and the Ghent varieties, are of large, beautiful and luxuriant bloom, and except the 'swamp honeysuckle' are the only azaleas hardy in western Massachusetts. Mollis is from two to six feet high, three to six feet broad, and blooms in April and May. Its blossoms are yellow, orange or pink, single or double. Its soil may be sandy or peaty, and moist, but any good garden soil will serve; its position partly shaded or in full sunlight. The Ghents are somewhat taller and not so broad in proportion. They bloom from May to July, and their blossoms are white, yellow, orange, pink, carmine, or red, single or double. Soil and position about the same as for mollis.

"Berberis. Berberis is the barberry, so well known by its beautiful pendent berries. It is one of the best shrubs to use where a thorny bush is wanted. B. vulgaris, the common sort, and one of the most beautiful, grows from four to eight feet high, with a breadth of from three to six feet. B. Thunbergii, or Thunberg's barberry, is the well-known Japanese variety, a dense, drooping bush from two to four feet high and somewhat greater breadth. Its pale-yellow blossoms come in April and May, and its small, slender, bright-red berries remain on the spray until spring. A dry soil is the best for it, though it will grow in any, and needs little shade or none. B. purpurea is a variety of vulgaris and is as handsome as the common. It answers to the same description, except that its foliage is purple, which makes it very tempting to new gardeners, but very hard to relate in good artistic taste among the other shrubs of the garden. Few small gardens can make good use of purple foliage.

"Deutzia gracilis. The gracilis is one of the most beautiful of all the deutzias. Its delicate foliage of rather light green, its snowy flowers and its somewhat bending form, make it one of the fairest ornaments of the home grounds. Its height is three feet, its breadth from two to four feet. It blooms in May and June. Its soil may be any well-drained sort, and its position any slightly sheltered aspect."

So we hurry down the alphabet. The list is short for several good reasons, one being that it is well to give other lists from season to season. No doubt our inaccuracies would distress a botanist or scientific gardener, but we convey the information, such as it is, to our fellow citizens, and they use it. In the last ten years we have furnished to our amateurs thousands of shrubs and plants, at the same reduced rates for a few specimens each which we pay for them by the hundred.

But of the really good sorts are there shrubs enough, you ask, to afford new lists year after year? Well, for the campus of a certain preparatory school for boys, with the planting of which the present writer had somewhat to do a few years ago, the list of shrubs set round the bases of four large buildings and several hundred yards of fence numbered seventy-five kinds. To end the chapter, let us say something about that operation. On a pictorial page or two we give ourselves the pleasure of showing the results of this undertaking; but first, both by pictures and by verbal description let me show where we planted what. Of course we made sundry mistakes. Each thing we did may be vulnerable to criticism, and our own largest hope is that our results may not fall entirely beneath that sort of compliment.

This campus covers some five acres in the midst of a small town. Along three of its boundaries old maples and elms, in ordinary single-file shade-tree lines, tower and spread. On the fourth line, the rear bound, a board fence divides the ground from the very unattractive back yards, stables and sheds of a number of town residents. The front lies along the main street of the place, facing the usual "shop-row." The entire area has nearly always been grassed. Not what an Englishman would call so, but turfed in a stuttering fashion, impetuous and abashed by turns, and very easy to keep off; most rank up against the granite underpinnings of the buildings, and managing somehow to writhe to all the fences, of which those on the street fronts are of iron. Parallel with the front fence and some fifty feet behind it, three of the institution's buildings stand abreast and about a hundred feet apart. All three are tall, rectangular three-story piles of old red brick, on granite foundations, and full of windows all of one size, pigeon-house style. The middle one has a fairly good Greek-pillared porch, of wood, on the middle half of its front.

Among these buildings we began our planting. We had drawn, of course, a ground plan of the whole place, to scale, showing each ground-floor door and window, so that we might respect its customary or projected use. A great point, that, in Where to Plant

What. I once heard of a school whose small boys were accused of wantonly trampling down some newly set shrubs on the playground. "Well," demanded one brave urchin, "what made 'em go and plant a lot of bushes right on first base?" And no one was ready with an answer, for there is something morally wrong about any garden that will rob a boy of his rights.

With this ground plan before us we decided indoors where to plant what outdoors and calculated arithmetically the number of each sort of shrub we should need for the particular interval we designed that sort to fill. Our scheme of arrangement was a crescendo of foliage and flower effects, beginning on the fronts of the buildings and rising toward their rears, while at all points making more of foliage than of bloom, because the bloom shows for only a month or less, while the leaf remains for seven or more. Beginning thus with our quietest note, the interest of any one looking in, or coming in, from the public front is steadily quickened and progressively rewarded, while the crowning effects at the rear of the buildings are reserved for the crowning moment when the visitor may be said to be fully received. On the other hand, if the approach is a returning one from the rear of the entire campus,—where stands the institution's only other building, a large tall-towered gymnasium, also of red brick,—these superlative effects show out across an open grassy distance of from two hundred to three hundred feet.

Wherefore—and here at last we venture to bring names of things and their places together—at the fronts of the northernmost and southernmost of these three "Halls" we set favorite varieties of white-flowering spireas (Thunbergia, sorbifolia, arguta, Van Houttei), the pearl-bush (exochorda), pink diervillas, and flowering-almonds. After these, on the southern side of the southernmost building, for example, followed lilacs, white and purple, against the masonry,—the white against the red brick, the lilac tint well away from it,—with tamarisk and kerria outside, abreast of them, and then pink and red spireas (Bumaldi and its dwarf variety, Anthony Waterer). On the other side of the same house we set deutzias (scabra against the brick-work and Lemoynei and gracilis outside). In a wing corner, where melting snows crash down from a roof-valley, we placed the purple-flowered Lespedeza penduliflorum, which each year dies to the ground before the snow-slides come, yet each September blooms from three to four feet high in drooping profusion. Then from that angle to the rear corner we put in a mass of pink wild roses. Lastly, on the tall, doorless, windowless rear end, we planted the crimson-rambler rose, and under it a good hundred of the red rugosas.

In the arrangement of these plantings we found ourselves called upon to deal with a very attractive and, to us, new phase of our question. The rising progression from front to rear was a matter of course, but how about the progression at right angles to it; from building to building, that is, of these three so nearly alike in size and dignity? To the passer-by along their Main Street front—the admiring passer-by, as we hope—should there be no augmentation of charm in the direction of his steps? And if there should be, then where and how ought it to show forth so as to avoid an anticlimax to one passing along the same front from the opposite direction? We promptly saw,—as the reader sees, no doubt, before we can tell it,—that what we wanted was two crescendos meeting somewhere near the middle; a crescendo passing into a diminuendo from whichever end you moved to the other—a swell. We saw that our loud-pedal effect should come upon "Middle Hall." So there, on its lucky bit of Greek porch, we bestowed the purple wistaria for spring, and for late summer that fragrant snowdrift, the clematis paniculata, so adapted as to festoon and chaplet, but never to smother, the Greek columns. On one of this structure's sides we planted forsythia, backed closer against the masonry by althæas, with the low and exquisite mahonia (holly-leafed barberry) under its outer spread. On the other side of the house we placed, first, loniceras (bush honeysuckles); next, azaleas, in variety and profusion; then, toward the rear end, a mass of hardy hydrangeas (Hydrangea paniculata grandiflora), and at the very back of the pile another mass, of the flowering-quince (Pyrus japonica), with the trumpet-creeper (Tecoma radicans), to climb out of it.

About "North Hall," the third building, we planted more quietly, and most quietly on its outer, its northern, side where our lateral "swell" (rising effect) begins, or ends, according to the direction of your going, beginning with that modest but pretty bloomer the Ligustrum ibota, a perfectly hardy privet more graceful than the California (ovalifolium) species, which really has little business in icy New England away from the seashore.

I might have remarked before that nearly all the walls of these three buildings, as well as the gymnasium on the far side of the campus, were already adorned with the "Boston ivy" (Ampelopsis Veitchii). With the plantings thus described, and with the gymnasium surrounded by yet stronger greenery; with the back fence masked by willows, elders and red-stemmed cornus; and with a number of haphazard footpaths reduced to an equally convenient and far more graceful few, our scheme stands complete in its first, but only, please notice, its first, phase. The picture is submitted to your imagination not as it looked the day we ceased planting, but as we expected it to appear after a season or two, and as it does look now.

At present, rather tardily, we have begun to introduce herbaceous flowering perennials, which we ignored in the first part of our plan, because herbaceous plants are the flesh and blood and garments of a complete living and breathing garden; the walls, shrubs, trees, walks and drives are its bones. When this secondary phase has been more fully realized and we have placed bush-clumps and tree-clumps out on the open campus, and when our hundreds of cottage gardens are shaking off the prison irons of frost, we hope, if you cannot do us the honor to be with us bodily, your spirit may be near, aiding us on in the conquest of this ever beautiful Where-to-Plant-What problem, which I believe would make us a finer and happier nation if it could be expanded to national proportions.

THE COTTAGE GARDENS OF NORTHAMPTON

Adam and Eve, it is generally conceded, were precocious. They entered into the cares and joys of adult life at an earlier age than any later human prodigy. We call them the grand old gardener and his wife, but, in fact, they were the youngest gardeners the world has ever seen, and they really did not give entire satisfaction. How could they without tools?

Let it pass. The whole allusion is prompted only by the thought that youth does not spontaneously garden. If it was actually necessary that our first parents should begin life as gardeners, that fully explains why they had to begin it also as adults. Youth enjoys the garden, yes! but not its making or tending. Childhood, the abecedarian, may love to plant seeds, to watch them spring, grow, and flower, and to help them do so; but that is the merest a-b-c of gardening, and no more makes him an amateur in the art than spelling words of one letter makes him a poet. One may raise or love flowers for a lifetime, yet never in any art sense become a gardener.

In front of the main building of a public institution which we must presently mention again there is a sloping strip of sward a hundred feet long and some fifteen wide. A florist of fully half a century's experience one day halted beside it and exclaimed to the present writer, "Only say the word, and I'll set out the 'ole len'th o' that strip in foliage-plants a-spellin' o' the name: 'People's Hinstitute!'" Yet that gentle enthusiast advertised himself as a landscape-gardener and got clients. For who was there to tell them or him that he was not one?

Not only must we confess that youth does not spontaneously garden, but that our whole American civilization is still so lingeringly in its non-gardening youth that only now and then, here and there, does it realize that a florist, whether professional or amateur, or even a nurseryman, is not necessarily a constructive gardener, or that artistic gardening, however informal, is nine-tenths constructive.

Yet particularly because such gardening is so, and because some of its finest rewards are so slow-coming and long-abiding, there is no stage of life in which it is so reasonable for man or woman to love and practise the art as when youth is in its first full stature and may garden for itself and not merely for posterity. "John," said his aged father to one of our living poets, "I know now how to transplant full-grown trees successfully. Do it a long time ago." Let the stripling plant the sapling.

Youth, however, and especially our American youth, has his or her excuses, such as they are. Of the garden or the place to be gardened, "It's not mine," he or she warmly says; "it's only my father's," or "my mother's."

Young man! Young maiden! True, the place, so pathetically begging to be gardened, may not be your future home, may never be your property, and it is right enough that a feeling for ownership should begin to shape your daily life. But let it not misshape it. You know that ownership is not all of life nor the better half of it, and it is quite as good for you to give the fact due recognition by gardening early in life as it was for Adam and Eve.

It is better, for you can do so in a much more fortunate manner, having tools and the first pair's warning example. It is better also because you can do what to them was impossible; you can make gardening a concerted public movement.

That is what we have made it in Northampton, Massachusetts, whose curving streets and ancient elms you may have heard of as making it very garden-like in its mere layout; many of whose windows, piazzas, and hillside lawns look on across the beautiful Connecticut, winding broadly among its farmed meadows and vanishing southward through the towering gateway made for or by it millenniums ago between Mounts Tom and Holyoke.

There Smith College is, as well as that "People's Institute" aforementioned, and it is through that institute, one of whose several branches of work is carried on wholly by Smith College students, that we, the Northampton townspeople, established and maintain another branch, our concerted gardening.

One evening in September a company of several hundred persons gathered in the main hall of the institute's "Carnegie House" to witness and receive the prize awards of their twelfth annual flower-garden competition.

The place was filled. A strong majority of those present were men and women who earn their daily bread with their hands. The whole population of Northampton is but twenty thousand or so, and the entire number of its voters hardly exceeds four thousand, yet there were one thousand and thirteen gardens in the competition, the gardens of that many homes; and although children had taken part in the care of many of them, and now were present to see the prizes go to their winners, not one was separately a child's garden. By a rule of the contest, each garden had been required to comprise the entire home lot, with the dwelling for its dominating feature and the family its spiritual unit.

The ceremony of award began with the lowest cash prize and moved steadily up to the second and first, these two being accompanied by brilliantly illuminated diplomas, and as each award was bestowed, the whole gathering of winners and non-winners—for no one could be called a loser—sounded their congratulations by a hearty clapping of hands. They had made the matter a public, concerted movement, and were interested in its results and rewards as spiritual proprietors in a common possession much wider than mere personal ownership under the law.

This wider sentiment of community, so valuable to the whole public interest, was further promoted by the combining of nearly two hundred of these same gardens in "neighborhood garden clubs" of seven or more gardens each, every garden in each club directly adjoining another, and the clubs competing for prizes of so much a garden to the best and second-best clubs.

Yet none the less for all this, but much more, a great majority of the multitude of home gardeners represented by this gathering were enjoying also—each home pair through their own home garden—the pleasures of personal ownership and achievement.

Many of the prize-winners were young, but many were gray, and some were even aged, yet all alike would have testified that even for age, and so all the more for youth, artistic flower-gardening is as self-rewarding a form of unselfish work and as promptly rewarding a mode of waiting on the future as can easily be found; that there is no more beautifully rewarding way by which youth may

"Learn to labor and to wait."

Maybe that is why Adam and Eve were apprenticed to it so very young.

It should have been said before that in advance of the award of prizes some very pleasant music and song were given from the platform by a few Smith College girls, and that then the company were shown stereopticon pictures of a number of their own gardens as they looked during the past summer and as they had looked when, a few years ago,—although seemingly but yesterday,—their owners began to plan and to plant.

The contrasts were amazing and lent great emphasis to the two or three truths we have here dwelt on probably long enough. To wit: first, that, as a rule, all true gardeners are grown-ups; second, that therein lies the finest value of concerted gardening; third, that the younger the grown-up the better, for the very reason that the crowning recompenses of true gardening come surely, but come late; and fourth, that, nevertheless, gardening yields a lovely amplitude of immediate rewards.

For instance, this gathering in our People's Institute also, before the announcement of prizes, took delight in hearing reported the aggregate of the flowers, mostly of that season's planting, distributed by a considerable number of the competitors to the shut-in and the bereaved. This feature of the movement had been begun only the previous year, and its total was no more than some three thousand dozens of flowers; but many grateful acknowledgments, both verbal and written, prove that it gave solace and joy to many hearts and we may call it a good beginning.

A garden should be owned not to be monopolized, but to be shared, as a song is owned not to be hushed, but to be sung; and the wide giving of its flowers is but one of several ways in which a garden may sing or be sung—for the garden is both song and singer. At any rate it cannot help but be a public benefaction and a public asset, if only its art be true.

Hence one of the values of our gardening in Northampton: making the gardens so many and so artistically true and good, it makes the town, as a whole, more interesting and pleasing to itself, and in corresponding degree the better to live in. Possibly there may be some further value in telling here how we do it.

As soon as signs of spring are plain to the general eye the visiting for enrolment begins. A secretary of the institute sets out to canvass such quarters of the field as have not been apportioned among themselves individually by the ladies composing the committee of "volunteer garden visitors." At the same time these ladies begin their calls, some undertaking more, some less, according to each one's willingness or ability.

This first round consists merely in enrolling the competitors by name, street, and number and in sending these registrations in to the institute. Later, by the same ladies, the same ground is more or less gone over again in visits of observation, inquiry and counsel, and once a month throughout the season the ladies meet together with the president of the institute to report the conditions and sentiments encountered and to plan further work.

The importance of these calls is not confined to the advancement of good gardening. They promote fellowship among neighbors and kind feeling between widely parted elements of society. Last year this committee made nearly eleven hundred such visits.

Meanwhile a circular letter has been early mailed to the previous year's competitors, urging them to re-enroll by post-card. Last year hundreds did so. Meanwhile, too, as soon as the enrolment is completed, the institute's general secretary begins a tour of official inspection, and as he is an experienced teacher of his art, his inspections are expert. His errand is known by the time he is in sight, and, as a rule, the householder joins him in a circuit of the place, showing achievements, reciting difficulties and disappointments, confessing errors, and taking tactful advice.

And what room he finds for tact! He sees a grave-like bed of verbenas defacing the middle of a small greensward—a dab of rouge on a young cheek; a pert child doing all the talking. Whereupon he shrewdly pleads not for the sward but for the flowers, "You have those there to show off at their best?"

"Yes. Don't they do it?"

"Not quite." He looks again. "Nine feet long—five wide. If you'll plant them next year in a foot-wide ribbon under that border of stronger things along your side boundary they'll give you at least forty feet of color instead of nine, and they'll illuminate your bit of sward instead of eclipsing it."

In another garden he says, "Splendid sunburst of color, that big tub of geraniums!" and the householder is pleased to admit the fact. "If you'd sink the tub into the ground clear down to the rim they'd take up no more room and they'd look natural. Besides, you wouldn't have to water them continually."

"That's true!" says the householder, quite in the incredible way of an old-fashioned book. "I'll do it!"

"And then," says the caller, "if you will set it away off on that far corner of the lawn it will shine clear across, showing everything between here and there, like a lighthouse across a harbor, or like a mirror, which you hang not in your parlor door, but at the far end of the room."

"When you come back you shall see it there," is the reply.

Sometimes, yet not often, a contestant is met who does not want advice, and who can hardly hide his scorn for book statements and experts. The present writer came upon one last year who "could not see what beauty there was in John Smith's garden, yet we had given him and his wife the capital prize!"

Frequently one finds the house of a competitor fast locked and dumb, its occupants being at work in some mill or shop. Then if the visit is one of official inspection a card stating that fact and dated and signed on the spot is left under the door, and on its reverse side the returning householder finds printed the following:

"In marking for merit your whole place is considered your garden. It is marked on four points: (1) Its layout, or ground plan; (2) its harmonies—of arrangement as to color of blooms and as to form and size of trees, shrubs and plants; (3) its condition—as to the neatness and order of everything; and (4) its duration—from how early in the year to how late it will make a pleasing show.

"Mow your lawn as often as the mower will cut the grass, but also keep it thoroughly weeded. As a rule, in laying out your plantings avoid straight lines and hard angles; the double curve, or wave line, is the line of grace. Plant all the flowers you wish, few or many, but set shrubs at their back to give stronger and more lasting effects when the flowers are out of season as well as while they are in bloom.

"Try to plant so as to make your whole place one single picture of a home, with the house the chief element and the boundary-lines of the lot the frame. Plant on all your lot's boundaries, plant out the foundation-lines of all its buildings; but between these plantings keep the space grassed only, and open. In these house and boundary borders let your chief plantings be shrubs, and so have a nine months' instead of a three months' garden."

The secretary's tour completed and his score of all the gardens tabulated, a list is drawn from it of the one hundred and fifty best gardens, and a second circuit of counsel and inspection, limited to this greatly reduced number, is made by the president of the institute, who marks them again on the same four points of merit.

These two markings, averaged, determine the standing of all prize-winning gardens except the leading four. Then the president calls in one professional and one amateur expert, visits with them as many of the most promising contestants as can be seen in an afternoon's drive, and with them decides the award of the four highest prizes.

That is all. When we have given two or three lesser items our story is told—for what it is worth. It is well to say we began small; in our first season, fifteen years ago, our whole roll of competitors numbered but sixty. It is the visiting that makes the difference; last season these visits, volunteer and official, were more than thirty-one hundred.

Another source of our success we believe to be the fact that our prizes are many and the leading ones large—fifteen, twelve, nine dollars, and so on down. Prizes and all, the whole movement costs a yearly cash outlay of less than three hundred dollars; without the People's Institute at its back it could still be done for five hundred.

And now, this being told in the hope that it may incite others, and especially youth, to make experiments like it elsewhere, to what impulse shall we appeal?

Will it not suffice if we invoke that adolescent instinct which moves us to merge our individual life—to consolidate it, as the stock-manipulators say—in the world's one great life, our "celestial selfishness" being intuitively assured that our own priceless individuality will gain, not lose, thereby?

Or shall we make our plea to an "art impulse"? No? Is the world already artificial enough? Not by half, although it is full, crammed, with the things the long-vanished dead have done for it in every art, from cameos to shade-trees; done for it because it was already so fair that, live long or die soon, they could not hold themselves back from making it fairer.

Yet, all that aside, is not this concerted gardening precisely such a work that young manhood and womanhood, however artificial or unartificial, anywhere, everywhere, Old World or newest frontier, ought to take to naturally? Adam and Eve did, and they—but we have squeezed Adam and Eve dry enough.

Patriotism! Can you imagine a young man or woman without it? And if you are young and a lover of your country, do you not love its physical aspects, "its rocks and rills, its woods and templed hills"? And if so, do you love only those parts of it which you never see and the appearance of which you have no power to modify? Or do you love the land only and not the people, the nation, the government? Or, loving these, have you no love for the nearest public fraction of it, your own town and neighbors? Why, then, your love of the Stars and Stripes is the flattest, silliest idolatry; so flat and silly it is hardly worth chiding. Your patriotism is a patriotism for war only, and a country with only that kind is never long without war.

You see the difference? Patriotism for war generalizes. A patriotism for peace particularizes, localizes. Ah, you do love, despite all their faults, your nation, your government, your town and townspeople, else you would not so often scold them! Otherwise, why do you let us call them yours? Because they belong to you? No, because you belong to them. Beyond cavil you are your own, but beyond cavil, too, you are theirs; their purchased possession, paid for long, long in advance and sight-unseen.

You cannot use a sidewalk, a street-lamp, or a post-box, or slip away into the woods and find them cleared of savages and deadly serpents, without seeing part of the price paid for you before your great-grandfather was born. So, then, loving your town enough to scold it, you will also serve it!

Now this we say not so much to be preaching as to bring in a last word descriptive of our Northampton movement. We do not make that work a mere aggregation of private kindnesses, but a public business for the promotion of the town in sanitary upkeep, beauty and civic fellowship.

And so our aim is not chiefly to reward the highest art in

gardening, but to procure its widest and most general dissemination. The individual is definitely subordinated to the community's undivided interest. Since gardening tends to develop in fortunate sections and to die out in others, we have laid off our town map in seven parts and made a rule that to each of these shall go three of the prizes.

Moreover, no two consecutive prizes can be awarded in any one of these districts. Where a competitor takes the capital prize no other can take a higher than the third, and if two in one district win the first and third prizes no one else there can take a higher than the fifth. So on through to prize twenty-one.

Still further, a garden taking any of these prizes can never again take any of them but a higher one, and those who attain to the capital prize are thenceforth hors concours except to strive for the "Past Competitors' Prizes," first and second.

Thus the seasons come and go, the gardens wake, rise, rejoice and slumber again; and because this arrangement is so evidently for the common weal and fellowship first, and yet leaves personal ownership all its liberties, rights and delights, it is cordially accepted of the whole people. And, lastly, as a certain dear lady whom we may not more closely specify exclaimed when, to her glad surprise, she easily turned the ceremonial golden key which first unlocked the Carnegie House of our People's Institute, "It works!"

THE PRIVATE GARDEN'S PUBLIC VALUE

What its pages are to a book, a town's private households are to a town.

No true home, standing solitarily apart from the town (unbound, as it were) could be the blessed thing it is were there not so many other houses not standing apart but gathered into villages, towns and cities.

Whence comes civilization but from civitas, the city? And where did civitas get its name, when city and state were one, but from citizen? He is not named for the city but the city for him, and his title meant first the head of a household, the master of a home. To make a civilization, great numbers of men must have homes, must mass them compactly together and must not mass them together on a dead level of equal material equipment but in a confederation of homes of all ranks and conditions.

The home is the cornerstone of the state.

The town, the organized assemblage of homes, is the keystone of civilization's arch.

In order to keep our whole civilization moving on and up, which is the only way for home and town to pay to each other their endless spiral of reciprocal indebtedness, every home in a town—or state, for that matter—should be made as truly and fully a home as every wise effort and kind influence of all the other homes can make it. Unless it takes part in this effort and influence, no home, be it ever so favored, can realize, even for itself and in itself, the finest civilization it might attain. Why should it? I believe this is a moral duty, a debt as real as taxes and very much like them.

In our People's Institute over in Northampton, Massachusetts, this is the a-b-c of all they seek to do: the individual tutoring, by college girls and town residents, of hundreds of young working men and women in whatever these may choose from among a score or so of light studies calculated to refine their aspirations; the training of young girls, by paid experts, in the arts of the home, from cooking to embroidery; the training of both sexes in all the social amenities; and the enlistment of more than a thousand cottage homes in a yearly prize competition.

It is particularly of this happy garden contest that I wish to say a word or two more. In 1914 it completed its sixteenth season, but it is modelled on a much older one in the town of Dunfermline, Scotland, the birthplace of Mr. Andrew Carnegie, and it is from the bountiful spirit of that great citizen of two lands that both affairs draw at least one vital element of their existence.

We in Northampton first learned of the Dunfermline movement in 1898. We saw at once how strongly such a scheme might promote the general spiritual enrichment of our working people's homes if made one of the functions of our home-culture clubs, several features of whose work were already from five to ten years old. We proceeded to adopt and adapt the plan, and had our first competition and award of prizes in 1898-'99.

Like Dunfermline, we made our prizes large, and to this we attribute no small part of our success. When we saw fit to increase their number we increased the total outlay as well, and at present we award twenty-one prizes a year, the highest being fifteen dollars, and one hundred dollars the sum of the whole twenty-one prizes. So we have gained one of our main purposes: to tempt into the contest the man of the house and thus to stimulate in him that care and pride of his home, the decline of which, in the man of the house, is one of the costliest losses of hard living.

One day on their round of inspection our garden judges came to a small house at the edge of the town, near the top of a hill through which the rustic street cuts its way some twelve or fifteen feet below. The air was pure, the surroundings green, the prospect wide and lovely. Here was a rare chance for picturesque gardening. Although the yard was without a fence there had been some planting of flowers in it. Yet it could hardly be called a garden. So destitute was it of any intelligent plan and so uncared for that it seemed almost to have a conscious, awkward self-contempt. In the flecked shade of a rude trellis of grapes that sheltered a side door two children of the household fell to work with great parade at a small machine, setting bristles into tooth-brushes for a neighboring factory, but it was amusingly plain that their labor was spasmodic and capricious.

The mother was away on a business errand. The father was present. He had done his day's stint in the cutlery works very early, and with five hours of sunlight yet before him had no use to make of them but to sit on a bowlder on the crest of the pleasant hill and smoke and whittle. Had he been mentally trained he might, without leaving that stone, have turned those hours into real living, communing with nature and his own mind; but he had, as half an eye could see, no developed powers of observation, reflection or imagination, and probably, for sheer want of practice, could not have fixed his attention on a worthy book through five of its pages. The question that arose in the minds of his visitors comes again here: what could have been so good to keep idleness from breeding its swarm of evils in his brain and hands—and home—as for somebody, something, somehow, to put it into his head—well—for example—to make a garden? A garden, we will say, that should win a prize, and—even though it failed to win—should render him and his house and household more interesting to himself, his neighbors and his town.

He and his house seemed to be keeping the Ten Commandments in a slouching sort of way and we may even suppose they were out of debt—money debt; yet already they were an unconscious menace to society; their wage-earning powers had outgrown their wants. Outgrown them not because the wages were too high but because their wants were too low; were only wants of the body, wants of the barrenest unculture; the inelastic wants.

That is "my own invention," that phrase! The bodily wants of a reptile are elastic. If an alligator or a boa-constrictor catches a dog he can swallow him whole and enjoy that one meal in unriotous bliss for weeks. Thereafter if he must put up with no more than a minnow or a mouse he can do that for weeks in unriotous patience. In a spring in one of our Northampton gardens I saw a catfish swallow a frog so big that the hind toes stuck out of the devourer's mouth for four days; but they went in at last, and the fish, in his fishy fashion, from start to finish was happy. He was never demoralized. It is not so with us. We cannot much distend or contract our purely physical needs. Especially is any oversupply of them mischievous. They have not the reptilian elasticity. Day by day they must have just enough. But the civilized man has spiritual wants and they are as elastic as air.

A home is a house well filled with these elastic wants. Home-culture is getting such wants into households—not merely into single individuals—that lack them. What makes a man rich? Is the term merely comparative? Not merely. To be rich is to have, beyond the demands of our bodily needs, abundant means to supply our spiritual wants. To possess more material resources than we can or will use or bestow to the spiritual advantage of ourselves and others is to be perilously rich, whether we belong to a grinders' union in the cutlery works or to a royal family. Why is it so often right that a rich college, for example, should, in its money-chest, feel poor? Because it could so easily supply more spiritual wants if it had more money.

Not low wages will ever make men harmless, nor high wages make them happy, nor low nor high save them from a spirit of pauperism or of malignant envy; but having wages bigger than their bodily wants, and having spiritual wants numerous and elastic enough to use up the surplus—spiritual wants, that know both how to suffer need and how to abound, and to do either without backsliding toward savagery. Whoever would help this state of things on, let him seek at the same time to increase the home's wage-earning power and its spiritual powers to put to fine use the wages earned: to augment the love of beauty in nature and in art, the love of truth and knowledge, the love of achievement and of service, the love of God and of human society, the ambition to put more into the world than we get out of it. Wages will never be too high, nor the hours of a day's work too many or too few, which follow that "sliding scale." How much our garden contest may do of this sort for that cottage on the hill we have yet to know; last year was its first in the competition. But it has shown the ambition to enter the lists, and a number that promised no more at the outset have since won prizes. One such was so beautiful last year that strangers driving by stopped and asked leave to dismount and enjoy a nearer view.

A certain garden to which we early awarded a high prize was, and yet remains, among the loveliest in Northampton. Its house stands perhaps seventy feet back from the public way and so nearly at one edge of its broad lot that all its exits and entrances are away from that side and toward the garden. A lawn and front bordered on side by loose hedges of Regel's privet and Thunberg's barberry and with only one or two slim trees of delicate foliage near its street line, rises slightly from the sidewalk to the house in a smooth half wave that never sinks below any level it has attained and yet consists of two curves. (It takes two curves, let us say once more, to make even half of the gentlest wave that can be made, if you take it from the middle of the crest to the middle of the trough, and in our American gardening thousands of lawns, especially small front lawns, are spoiled in their first layout by being sloped in a single curve instead of in two curves bending opposite ways.) Along a side of this greensward farthest from the boundary to which the house is so closely set are the drive and walk, in one, and on the farther side of these, next the sun, is the main flower-garden, half surrounding another and smaller piece of lawn. The dwelling stands endwise to the street and broadside to this expanse of bloom. Against its front foundations lies a bed of flowering shrubs which at the corner farthest from the drive swings away along that side's boundary line and borders it with shrubbery down to the street, the main feature of the group being a luxuriant flowering quince as large as ten ordinary ones and in every springtime a red splendor.

But the focus of the gardening scheme is at the southeasterly side entrance of the house. To this the drive comes on unrigorous lines from the street. The walk curves away a few steps earlier to go to the front door but the drive, passing on, swings in under the rear corner windows and to the kitchen steps, veers around by the carriage-house door and so loops back into itself. In this loop, and all about the bases of the dwelling and carriage-house the flowers rise in dense abundance, related to one another with clever taste and with a happy care for a procession of bloom uninterrupted throughout the season. Straightaway from the side door, leaving the drive at a right angle, runs a short arbor of vines. Four or five steps to the left of this bower a clump of shrubbery veils the view from the street and in between shrubs and arbor lies a small pool of water flowers and goldfish. On the arbor's right, in charming privacy, masked by hollyhocks, dahlias and other tall-maidenly things, lie beds of strawberries and lettuce and all the prim ranks and orders of the kitchen garden.

Words are poor things to paint with; I wish I could set forth all in one clear picture: lawn, drive, house, loop, lily pond, bower, rose-bordered drive again (as the eye comes back) and flowers crowding before, behind and beside you, some following clear out to the street and beseeching you not to go so soon. Such is the garden, kept without hired labor, of two soft-handed women; not beyond criticism in any of its aspects but bearing witness to their love of nature, of beauty and of home and of their wisdom and skill to exalt and refine them.

This competitor early won, I say, a leading prize, and in later seasons easily held—still holds—a fine pre-eminence. Yet the later prizes fell to others, because, while this one had been a beautiful garden for years before the competition began, they, rising from much newer and humbler beginnings, sometimes from very chaos, showed between one season and the next far greater advances toward artistic excellence. In the very next year a high prize fell to a garden in full sight of this one, a garden whose makers had caught their inspiration from this one, and, copying its art, had brought forth a charming result out of what our judges described as "particularly forlorn conditions."

Does this seem hardly fair to the first garden? But to spread the gardening contagion and to instigate a wise copying after the right gardeners—these are what our prizes and honors are for. Progress first, perfection afterward, is our maxim. We value and reward originality, nevertheless, and only count it a stronger necessity to see not merely that no talented or happily circumstanced few, but that not even any one or two fortunate neighborhoods, shall presently be capturing all the prizes. Hence the rules already cited, which a prompt discovery of this tendency forced upon us.

About this copying: no art is more inoffensively imitated than gardening but unluckily none is more easily, or more absurdly, miscopied. A safe way is to copy the gardener rather than the garden. To copy any performance in a way to do it honor we must discern and adapt its art without mimicking its act. To miscopy is far easier—we have only to mimic the act and murder the art. I once heard a man ask an architect if it would not answer to give his plan to the contractor and let him work it out without the architect's supervision.

"My dear sir," the architect replied, "you wouldn't know the corpse."

I suppose one reason why even the miscopying of gardens provokes so little offence is that the acts it mimics have no art it can murder. Mrs. Budd sets out her one little "high geraingia" in the middle of her tiny grass-plat (probably trimming it to look like a ballet-dancer on one leg). Whereupon Mrs. Mudd, the situation of whose house and grounds is not in the least like her neighbor's, plants and trims hers the same way and feels sure it has the same effect, for — why shouldn't it?

The prize-winning copyist I am telling of copied principles only. To have copied mere performance would have been particularly unlucky, for though his garden stands within fifty yards of the one from which it drew its inspiration the two are so differently located that the same art principles demand of them very different performances. An old-time lover of gardens whom I have to quote at second-hand mentions in contrast "gardens to look in upon" and "gardens to look out from." The garden I have described at length is planned to be looked in upon; most town gardens must be, of course; but its competitor across the street, of which I am about to give account, is an exception. The lot has a very broad front and very little depth — at one side almost none, at the other barely enough for a small house and a few feet of front yard. Why there should be a drive I cannot say, but it is so well taken into the general scheme that to call it to account would be ungenerous. It enters at the narrowest part of the ground, farthest from the house, makes a long parabola, and turns again into the street close beside the dwelling. In the bit of lawn thus marked off, shrubs have place near the street, three or four old apple-trees range down the middle, and along the drive runs a gay border of annual flowers. Along the rear side of the drive lies but a narrow strip of turf beyond which the ground drops all at once to another level some thirty feet below. On the right this fall is so abrupt that the only way down to it is by a steep rustic stair. On the left, behind the house, the face of the bluff is broken into narrow terraces, from top to bottom of which, and well out on the lower level, the entire space is mantled with the richly burdened trellises of a small vineyard. At the right on this lower ground is a kitchen garden; beyond it stretch fair meadows too low to build on, but fruitful in hay and grain; farther away, on higher ground, the town again shows its gables and steeples among its great maples and elms, and still beyond, some three miles distant, the green domes and brown precipices of the Mount Holyoke Range stand across the sky in sharp billows of forest and rock. It seems at times a pity that Mount Holyoke and Mount Tom cannot themselves know how many modest gardens they are a component part of—the high violin note of: gardens, like this one, "to look out from."

It stops one's pen for one to find himself using the same phrases for these New England cottage gardens that famous travellers have used in telling of the gardens of Italian princes; yet why should we not, when the one nature and the one art are mother and godmother of them all? It is a laughing wonder what beauty can be called into life about the most unpretentious domicile, out of what ugliness such beauty can be evoked and at how trivial a cost in money. Three years before this "garden to look out from" won its Carnegie prize it was for the most part a rubbish heap. Let me now tell of one other, that sprang from conditions still more unlovely because cramped and shut in.

It was on the other side of the town from those I have been telling of. The house stood broadside to the street and flush with the sidewalk. The front of the lot was only broad enough for the house and an alley hardly four feet wide between the house's end and a high, tight board fence. The alley led into a small, square back yard one of whose bounds was the back fence of the house. On a second side was a low, mossy, picturesquely old wing-building set at right angles to the larger house, its doors and windows letting into the yard. A third boundary was the side of one well weathered barn and the back of another, with a scanty glimpse between them of meadows stretching down to the Connecticut River. The fourth was an open fence marking off a field of riotous weeds. When the tenant mistress of this unpromising spot began to occupy it the yard and alley were a free range for the poultry of the neighborhood, and its only greenery was two or three haphazard patches of weedy turf. One-fourth of the ground, in the angle made by the open fence and one of the barns, had been a hen-yard and was still inclosed within a high wire-netting; but outside that space every plant she set out had to be protected from the grubbing fowls by four stakes driven down with a hammer. Three years afterward she bore off our capital prize in a competition of one hundred gardens. Let me tell what the judges found.

Out in the street, at the off side of the alley-gate, between a rude fence and an electric-railway siding, in about as much space as would give standing room to one horse and cart, bloomed—not by right of lease, but by permission of the railway company—a wealth of annual flowers, the lowest (pansies and such like) at the outer edge, the tallest against the unsightly fence. This was the prelude. In the alley the fence was clothed with vines; the windows—of which there were two—were decked with boxes of plumbago— pink, violet, white and blue, and of lady-ferns and maiden-hair. The back yard was a soft, smooth turf wherever there were not flowers.

Along the back doors and windows of the house and the low-roofed wing a rough arbor was covered with a vine whose countless blossoms scented the air and feasted the bees, while its luminous canopy sheltered a rare assemblage of such flowers as bloom and thrive only for those whom they know and trust. But the crowning transformation was out in the open sunlight, in the space which had been the hen-yard. Within it was a holiday throng of the gardening world's best-known and loved gentles and commons, from roses down to forget-me-nots. Its screen of poultry-netting had been kept in place, and no feature on the premises more charmingly showed that this floral profusion came of no mere greed for abundance or diversity, but of a true art instinct recognizing the limits of its resources. The garden had to be made a "garden to look in upon," a veritable imprisoned garden; the question of expense required it to be chiefly of annuals, and all the structural features of the place called for concealment. These wire nettings did so; on their outside, next the grass, two complete groups of herbaceous things were so disposed as to keep them veiled in bloom throughout the whole warm half of the year. Close against them and overpeering their tops were hollyhocks and dahlias; against these stood at lesser height sweet peas, asters, zinnias, coreopsis and others of like stature; in front of these were poppies for summer, marigolds for autumn; beneath these again were verbenas, candytuft—all this is sketched from memory, and I recall the winsome effect rather than species and names; and still below nestled portulaca and periwinkle. I fear the enumeration gives but a harlequin effect; but the fault of that is surely mine, for the result was delightful.

I have ventured to make report of these two or three gardens, not as in themselves worthy of a great public's consideration and praise but as happy instances of a fruitage we are gathering among hundreds of homes in a little city where it is proposed to give every home, if possible, its utmost value. Many other pleasing examples could be cited if further turnings of the kaleidoscope were a real need, but this slender discourse is as long now as it should be. It seems droll to call grave attention to such humble things in a world so rightly preoccupied with great sciences and high arts, vast industries, shining discoveries and international rivalries, strifes and projects; yet what are all these for, at last, but the simple citizen, his family and his home, and for him and them in the cottage as well as in the palace? The poor man's home may shine dimly but it is one of the stars by which civilization must guide its onward course.

It may well be supposed that those whose office it is to award the twenty-one prizes of our garden competition among our eleven hundred competitors have an intricate task. Yet some of its intricacies add to the pleasure of it.

One of these pleasing complications arises from our division of the field of contest into seven parts, in each of which prizes must be given to three contestants. Another comes from our rule that not alone the competitors who show the best gardening are to be rewarded, but also those who have made the most earnest effort and largest progress toward the best gardening. Under this plan one whose work shows a patient and signal progress in the face of many disadvantages may outrank on our prize list a rival whose superior artistic result has been got easily under favoring conditions and reveals no marked advance beyond the season before.

After the manner of Dunfermline again, our rules are that no gardener by trade and no one who hires help in his garden may compete. Any friend may help his friend, and any one may use all the advice he can get from amateur or professional. Children may help in the care of the gardens, and many do; but children may not themselves put gardens into the competition.

"If the head of the house is the gardener-in-chief," shrewdly argued one of our committee, "the children, oftener than otherwise, will garden with him, or will catch the gardening spirit as they grow up; but if the children are head-gardeners we shall get only children's gardening. We want to dispel the notion that flower-gardening is only woman's work and child's play."

Our rule against hired labor sets naturally a maximum limit to the extent of ground a garden may cover. Our minimum is but fifty square yards, including turf, beds, and walks, and it may be of any shape whatever if only it does not leave out any part of the dooryard, front or rear, and give it up to neglect and disorder. To the ear even fifty square yards seems extensive, but really it is very small. It had so formidable a sound when we first named it that one of our most esteemed friends, pastor of a Catholic church in that very pretty and thrifty part of Northampton called for its silk mills Florence, generously added two supplementary prizes for gardens under the limit of size. This happy thought had a good effect, for, although in the first and second years Father Gallon's people took prizes for gardens above the minimum limit in size, while his own two prizes fell to contestants not in his flock, yet only in the third year did it become to all of us quite as plain as a pikestaff that fifty square yards are only the one-fiftieth part of fifty yards square, and that whoever in Northampton had a dooryard at all had fifty square yards. In 1903 more than two hundred and fifty gardens were already in the contest but every one was large enough to compete for the Carnegie prizes, and the kind bestower of the extra ones (withdrawn as superfluous), unselfishly ignoring his own large share of credit, wrote:

"Your gardens have altered the aspect of my parish."

Such praise is high wages. It is better than to have achieved the very perfection of gardening about any one home. We are not trying to raise the world's standard of the gardening art. Our work is for the home and its indwellers; for the home and the town. Our ideal is a town of homes all taking pleasant care of one another. We want to make all neighbors and all homes esthetically interesting to one another, believing that this will relate them humanely, morally and politically. We began with those who pay no one to dig, plant or prune for them, but soon we went further and ventured to open to gardens kept with hired service an allied competition for a separate list of prizes. In this way we put into motion, between two elements of our people which there are always more than enough influences to hold sufficiently apart, a joint pursuit of the same refining delight and so promoted the fellowship of an unconflicting common interest. In degree some of us who use hired help had already obtained this effect. Last season:

"Come," I often heard one of our judges say on his rounds, "see my own garden some afternoon; I'll show you all the mistakes I've made!" And some came, and exchanged seeds and plants with him.

"A high civilization," said an old soldier to me only a few days ago, "must always produce great social inequalities. They are needed mainly by and for those who see no need of them."

I admitted that the need is as real, though not so stern, as the need of inequalities in military rank.

"But," I said, "in the military relation you must also vividly keep up, across all inequalities of rank, a splendid sentiment of common interest and devotion, mutual confidence and affection, or your army will be but a broken weapon, a sword without a hilt."

"Yes," he agreed, "and so in civilization; if it would be of the highest it must draw across its lines of social cleavage the bonds of civic fellowship."

It was what I had intended to say myself. Social selection raises walls between us which we all help to build, but they need not be Chinese walls. They need not be so high that civic fellowship, even at its most feminine stature, may not look over them every now and then to ask:

"How does my neighbor's garden grow?"

It is with this end in view as well as for practical convenience that we have divided our field into seven districts and from our "women's council" have appointed residents of each to visit, animate and counsel the contestants of that district. The plan works well.

On the other hand, to prevent the movement, in any district, from shrinking into village isolation; in order to keep the whole town comprised, and, as nearly as may be, to win the whole town's sympathy and participation, we have made a rule that in whatever district the capital prize is awarded, the second prize must go to some other district. If we have said this before you may slip it here; a certain repetitiousness is one part of our policy. A competitor in the district where the capital prize is awarded may take the third prize, but no one may take the third in the district where the second has been awarded. He may, however, be given the fourth. In a word, no two consecutive prizes can be won in the same district. Also, not more than three prizes of the fifteen may in one season be awarded in any one district. So each district has three prize-winners each year, and each year the prizes go all over town. Again, no garden may take the same prize two years in succession; it must take a higher one or else wait over.

"This prize-garden business is just all right!" said one of the competitors to our general secretary. "It gives us good things to say to one another's face instead of bad things at one another's back, it does!"

That is a merit we claim for it; that it operates, in the most inexpensive way that can be, to restore the social bond. Hard poverty minus village neighborship drives the social relation out of the home and starves out of its victims their spiritual powers to interest and entertain one another, or even themselves. If something could keep alive the good aspects of village neighborship without disturbing what is good in that more energetic social assortment which follows the expansion of the village into the town or city, we should have better and fairer towns and cities and a sounder and safer civilization. But it must be something which will give entirely differing social elements "good things to say to one another's face instead of bad things at one another's back."

We believe our Northampton garden competition tends to do this. It brings together in neighborly fellowship those whom the discrepancies of social accomplishments would forever hold asunder and it brings them together without forced equality or awkward condescension, civic partners in that common weal to neglect which is one of the "dangers and temptations of the home."

Two of our committee called one day at a house whose garden

seemed to have fallen into its ill condition after a very happy start. Its mistress came to the door wearing a heart-weary look. The weather had been very dry, she said in a melodious French accent, and she had not felt so very well, and so she had not cared to struggle for a garden, much less for a prize.

"But the weather," suggested her visitors, "had been quite as dry for her competitors, and few of them had made so fair a beginning. To say nothing of prizes, was not the garden itself its own reward?"

She shook her head drearily; she did not know that she should ever care to garden any more.

"Why?" exclaimed one questioner persuasively, "you didn't talk so when I was here last month!"

"No," was the reply, "but since three weeks ago—" and all at once up came the stifled tears, filling her great black eyes and coursing down her cheeks unhindered, "I los' my baby."

The abashed visitors stammered such apologies as they could. "They would not have come on this untimely errand could they have known." They begged forgiveness for their slowness to perceive.

"Yet do not wholly," they presently ventured to urge, "give up your garden. The day may come when the thought that is now so bitter will, as a memory, yield some sweetness as well, and then it may be that the least of bitterness and the most of sweetness will come to you when you are busy among your flowers."

"It may be," she sighed, but with an unconvinced shrug. And still, before the summer was gone, the garden sedately, yet very sweetly, smiled again and even the visitors ventured back.

That was nearly three years ago. Only a few weeks since those two were in the company of an accomplished man who by some chance—being a Frenchman—had met and talked with this mother and her husband.

"We made a sad bungle there," said the visitors.

"Do not think it!" he protested. "They are your devoted friends. They speak of you with the tenderest regard. Moreover, I think they told me that last year—"

"Yes," rejoined one of the visitors, "last year their garden took one of the prizes."

THE MIDWINTER GARDENS OF NEW ORLEANS

If the following pages might choose their own time and place they would meet their reader not in the trolley-car or on the suburban train, but in his own home, comfortably seated. For in order to justify the eulogistic tone of the descriptions which must presently occupy them their first word must be a conciliatory protest against hurry. One reason we Americans garden so little is that we are so perpetually in haste. The art of gardening is primarily a leisurely and gentle one.

And gentility still has some rights. Our Louisiana Creoles know this, and at times maintain it far beyond the pales of their evergreen gardens.

"'Step lively'?" one of them is said to have amazedly retorted in a New York street-car. "No, the lady shall not step lively. At yo' leisure, madame, entrez!" In New Orleans the conductors do not cry "Step lively!" Right or wrong, the cars there are not absolutely democratic. Gentility really enjoys in them a certain right to be treated gently.

If democracy could know its own tyrants it would know that one of them is haste—the haste, the hurry of the crowd; that hurry whose cracking whip makes every one a compulsory sharer in it. The street-car conductor, poor lad, is not to blame. The fault is ours, many of us being in such a scramble to buy democracy at any price that, as if we were belatedly buying railway tickets, we forget to wait for our change.

Now one of this tyrant's human forms is a man a part of whose tyranny is to call himself a gardener, though he knows he is not one, and the symbol of whose oppression is nothing more or less than that germ enemy of good gardening, the lawn-mower. You, if you know the gardening of our average American home almost anywhere else, would see, yourself, how true this is, were you in New Orleans. But you see it beautifully proved not by the presence but by the absence of the tyranny. The lawn-mower is there, of course; no one is going to propose that the lawn-mower anywhere be abolished. It is one of our modern marvels of convenience, a blessed release of countless human backs from countless hours of crouching, sickle-shaped, over the sickle. It is not the tyrant, but only like so many other instruments of beneficent democratic emancipation, the tyrant's opportunity. A large part of its convenience is expedition, and expedition is the easiest thing in the world to become vulgarized; vulgarized it becomes haste, and haste is the tyrant. Such arguing would sound absurdly subtle aimed against the uncloaked, barefaced tyranny of the street-car conductor, but the tyranny of the man with the lawn-mower is itself subtle, masked, and requires subtlety to unmask it.

See how it operates. For so we shall be the better prepared for a generous appreciation of those far Southern gardens whose beauty has singled them out for our admiration. We know, of course, that the "formal garden," by reason of its initial and continuing costliness, is, and must remain, the garden of the wealthy few, and that the gardening for the great democracy of our land, the kind that will make the country at large a gardened land, is "informal," freehand, ungeometrical gardening. In this sort, on whatever scale, whether of the capitalist or of the cottager, the supreme feature is the lawn; the lawn-mower puts this feature within the reach of all, and pretty nearly every American householder has, such as it is, his bit of Eden.

But just in that happy moment the Tempter gets in. The garden's mistress or master is beguiled to believe that one may have a garden without the expense of a gardener and at the same time without any gardening knowledge. The stable-boy, or the man-of-all-work, or the cook, or the cottager himself, pushes the lawn-mower, and except for green grass, or changeable brown and green, their bit of Eden is naked and is not ashamed.

Or if ashamed, certain other beguilements, other masked democratic tyrannies, entering, reassure it; bliss of publicity, contempt of skill, and joy in machinery and machine results. An itinerant ignoramus comes round with his own lawn-mower, the pushing of which he now makes his sole occupation for the green half of the year, and the entire length, breadth and thickness of whose wisdom is a wisdom not of the lawn but only of the lawn-mower; how to keep its bearings oiled and its knives chewing fine; and the lawn becomes staringly a factory product.

Then tyranny turns the screw again, and in the bliss of publicity and a very reasonable desire to make the small home lot look as large as possible, down come the fences, side and front, and the applauding specialist of the lawn-mower begs that those obstructions may never be set up again, because now the householder can have his lawn mowed so much quicker, and he, the pusher, can serve more customers. Were he truly a gardener he might know somewhat of the sweet, sunlit, zephyrous, fragrant outdoor privacies possible to a real garden, and more or less of that benign art which, by skilful shrubbery plantings, can make a small place look much larger—as well as incomparably more interesting—than can any mere abolition of fences, and particularly of the street fence. But he has not so much as one eye of a genuine gardener or he would know that he is not keeping your lawn but only keeping it shaven. He is not even a good garden laborer. You might as well ask him how to know the wild flowers as how to know the lawn pests—dandelion, chickweed, summer-grass, heal-all, moneywort and the like—with which you must reckon wearily by and by because he only mows them in his blindness and lets them flatten to the ground and scatter their seed like an infantry firing-line. Inquire of him concerning any one of the few orphan shrubs he has permitted you to set where he least dislikes them, and which he has trimmed clear of the sod—put into short skirts—so that he may run his whirling razors under (and now and then against) them at full speed. Will he know the smallest fact about it or yield any echo of your interest in it?

There is a late story of an aged mother, in a darkened room, saying falteringly to the kind son who has brought in some flowers which she caresses with her soft touch, "I was wishing to-day—We used to have them in the yard—before the lawn-mower—" and saying no more. I know it for a fact, that in a certain cemetery the "Sons of the American Revolution" have for years been prevented from setting up their modest marks of commemoration upon the graves of Revolutionary heroes, because they would be in the way of the sexton's lawn-mower.

Now in New Orleans the case is so different that really the amateur gardener elsewhere has not all his rights until he knows why it is so different. Let us, therefore, look into it. In that city one day the present writer accosted an Irishman who stood, pruning-shears in hand, at the foot of Clay's statue, Lafayette Square. It was the first week of January, but beside him bloomed abundantly that lovely drooping jasmine called in the books jasminum multiflorum.

"Can you tell me what shrub this is?"

"That, sor, is the monthly flora! Thim as don't know the but-hanical nayum sometimes calls it the stare jismin, but the but-hanical nayum is the monthly flora."

The inquirer spoke his thanks and passed on, but an eager footfall overtook him, his elbow felt a touch, and the high title came a third time: "The but-hanical nayum is the monthly flora."

The querist passed on, warmed by a grateful esteem for one who, though doubtless a skilled and frequent tinkler of the lawn-mower within its just limitations, was no mere dragoon of it, but kept a regard for things higher than the bare sod, things of grace in form, in bloom, in odor, and worthy of "but-hanical nayum." No mere chauffeur he, of the little two-wheeled machine whose cult, throughout the most of our land, has all but exterminated ornamental gardening.

In New Orleans, where it has not conquered, there is no crowding for room. A ten-story building is called there a sky-scraper. The town has not a dozen in all, and not one of that stature is an apartment or tenement house. Having felled her surrounding forests of cypress and drained the swamps in which they stood, she has at command an open plain capable of housing a population seven times her present three hundred and fifty thousand, if ever she chooses to build skyward as other cities do.

But this explains only why New Orleans might have gardens, not why she chooses to have them, and has them by thousands, when hundreds of other towns that have the room—and the lawns—choose not to have the shrubberies, vines and flowers, or have them without arrangement. Why should New Orleans so exceptionally choose to garden, and garden with such exceptional grace? Her house-lots are extraordinarily numerous in proportion to the numbers of her people, and that is a beginning of the explanation; but it is only a beginning. Individually the most of those lots are no roomier than lots elsewhere. Thousands of them, prettily planted, are extremely small.

The explanation lies mainly in certain peculiar limitations, already hinted, of her—democracy! That is to say, it lies in her fences. Her fences remain, her democracy is different from the Northern variety. The difference may consist only in faults both there and here which we all hope to see democracy itself one day eliminate; but the difference is palpable. The fences mean that the dwellers behind them have never accorded to each other, as neighbors, that liberty-to-take-liberties of which Northern householders and garden-holders, after a quarter-century's disappointing experiment, are a bit weary.

In New Orleans virtually every home, be it ever so proud or poor, has a fence on each of its four sides. As a result the home is bounded by its fences, not by its doors. Unpleasant necessities these barriers are admitted to be, and those who have them are quite right in not liking them in their bare anatomy. So they clothe them with shrubberies and vines and thus on the home's true corporate bound the garden's profile, countenance and character are established in the best way possible; without, that is, any impulse toward embellishment insulated from utility. Compelled by the common frailties of all human nature (even in a democracy) to maintain fortifications, the householder has veiled the militant aspect of his defences in the flowered robes and garlandries of nature's diplomacy and hospitality. Thus reassured, his own inner hospitality can freely overflow into the fragrant open air and out upon the lawn—a lawn whose dimensions are enlarged to both eye and mind, inasmuch as every step around its edges—around its meandering shrubbery borders—is made affable and entertaining by Flora's versatilities.

At the same time, let us note in passing, this enlargement is partly because the lawn—not always but very much oftener than where lawns go unenclosed—lies clean-breasted, green-breasted, from one shrub-and-flower-planted side to the other, along and across; free of bush, statue, urn, fountain, sun-dial or pattern-bed, an uninterrupted sward. Even where there are lapses from this delightful excellence they often do not spoil, but only discount, more or less, the beauty of the general scheme, as may be noted—if without offence we may offer it the homage of criticism—in one of the gardens we have photographed to illustrate these argumentations. There eight distinct encumbrances narrow the sward without in the least adding to the garden's abounding charm. The smallest effort of the reader's eye will show how largely, in a short half-day's work, the fair scene might be enhanced in lovely dignity simply by the elimination of these slight excesses, or by their withdrawal toward the lawn's margins and into closer company with the tall trees.

In New Orleans, where, even when there are basements, of which there are many, the domains of the cook and butler are somewhere else, a nearly universal feature of every sort of dwelling—the banker's on two or three lots, the laborer's on half a one—is a paved walk along one side of the house, between the house and the lawn, from a front gate to the kitchen. Generally there is but the one front gate, facing the front door, with a short walk leading directly up to this door. In such case the rear walk, beginning at the front door-steps, turns squarely along the house's front, then at its corner turns again as squarely to the rear as a drill-sergeant and follows the dwelling's ground contour with business precision—being a business path. In fact it is only the same path we see in uncrowded town life everywhere in our land.

But down there it shows this peculiarity, that it is altogether likely to be well bordered with blooming shrubs and plants along all that side of it next the lawn. Of course it is a fault that this shrubbery border—and all the more so because it is very apt to be, as in three of our illustrations a rose border—should, so often as it is, be pinched in between parallel edges. "No pinching" is as good a rule for the garden as for the kindergarten. Manifestly, on the side next the house the edge between the walk and the planted border should run parallel with the base line of the house, for these are business lines and therefore ever so properly lines of promptitude—of the shortest practicable distance between two points—lines of supply and demand, lines of need. For lines of need, business speed!

But for lines of pleasure, grace and leisure. It is the tactful office of this shrubbery border to veil the business path from the lawn—from the pleasure-ground. Therefore its outside, lawn-side edge should be a line of pleasure, hence a line of grace, hence not a straight line (dead line), nor yet a line of but one lethargic curve, but a line of suavity and tranquil ongoing, a leisurely undulating line.

Not to have it so is an error, but the error is an inoffensive one easily corrected and the merit is that the dwelling's business path is greenly, bloomingly screened from its pleasure-ground by a lovely natural drapery which at the same time furnishes, as far as the path goes, the house's robes of modesty. Indeed they are furnished farther than the path goes; for no good work gathers momentum more readily than does good gardening, and the householder, having begun so rightly, has now nothing to do to complete the main fabric of his garden but to carry this flow of natural draperies on round the domicile's back and farther side and forward to its front again. Thus may he wonderfully extenuate, even above its reach and where it does not conceal, the house's architectural faults, thus winsomely enhance all its architectural charm; like a sweet human mistress of the place, putting into generous shadow all the ill, and into open sunshine all the best, of a husband's strong character.

And now if this New Orleans idea—that enough private enclosure to secure good home gardening is not incompatible with public freedom, green lawns, good neighborship, sense of room and fulness of hospitality, and that a house-lot which is a picture is worth more to everybody (and therefore is even more democratic) than one which is little else than a map—if this idea, we say, finds any credence among sister cities and towns that may be able to teach the Creole city much in other realms of art and criticism, let us cast away chalk and charcoal for palette and brush and show in floral, arborescent, redolent detail what is the actual pictorial excellence of these New Orleans gardens.

For notwithstanding all their shut-in state, neither their virtues nor their faults are hid from the passing eye. The street fence, oftenest of iron, is rarely more than breast-high and is always an open fence. Against its inner side frequently runs an evergreen hedge never taller than the fence's top. Commonly it is not so tall, is always well clipped and is so civil to strangers that one would wish to see its like on every street front, though he might prefer to find it not so invariably of the one sort of growth—a small, handsome privet, that is, which nevertheless fulfils its office with the perfection of a solid line of palace sentries. Unluckily there still prevails a very old-fashioned tendency to treat the front fence as in itself ornamental and to forget two things: First, that its nakedness is no part of its ornamental value; that it would be much handsomer lightly clothed—underclothed—like, probably, its very next neighbor; clothed with a hedge, either close or loose, and generously kept below the passer's line of sight. And, second, that from the householder's point of view, looking streetward from his garden's inner depth, its fence, when unplanted, is a blank interruption to his whole fair scheme of meandering foliage and bloom which on the other three sides frames in the lawn; as though the garden were a lovely stage scene with the fence for footlights, and some one had left the footlights unlit.

A lovely stage scene, we say, without a hint of the stage's unreality; for the side and rear fences and walls, being frankly unornamental, call for more careful management than the front and are often charmingly treated. Where they separate neighbors' front lawns they may be low and open, but back of the building-line, being oftenest tight and generally more than head-high, they are sure to be draped with such climbing floral fineries as honeysuckles, ivies, jasmines white and yellow, lantanas, roses or the Madeira vine.

More frequently than not they are planted also, in strong masses, with ever so many beautiful sorts of firmer-stemmed growths, herbaceous next the sod, woody behind, assembled according to stature, from one to twelve feet high, swinging in and out around the lawn until all stiffness of boundaries is waved and smiled away.

In that first week of January already mentioned the present writer saw at every turn, in such borders and in leaf and blossom, the delicate blue-flowered plumbago; two or three kinds of white jasmine, also in bloom; and the broad bush-form of the yellow jasmine, beginning to flower. With them were blooming roses of a dozen kinds; the hibiscus (not althæa but the H. rosasinensis of our Northern greenhouses), slim and tall, flaring its mallow-flowers pink, orange, salmon and deep red; the trailing-lantana, covering broad trellises of ten feet in height and with its drooping masses of delicate foliage turned from green to mingled hues of lilac and rose by a complete mantle of their blossoms. He saw the low, sweet-scented geraniums of lemon, rose and nutmeg odors, persisting through the winter unblighted, and the round-leaved, "zonal" sorts surprisingly large of growth—in one case, on a division fence, trained to the width and height of six feet. There, too, was the poinsettia still bending in its Christmas red, taller than the tallest man's reach, often set too forthpushingly at the front, but at times, with truer art, glowing like a red constellation from the remoter bays of the lawn; and there, taller yet, the evergreen Magnolia fuscata, full of its waxen, cream-tinted, inch-long flowers smelling delicately like the banana. He found the sweet olive, of refined leaf and minute axillary flowers yielding their ravishing tonic odor with the reserve of the violet; the pittosporum; the box; the myrtle; the camphor-tree with its neat foliage answering fragrantly the grasp of the hand. The dark camellia was there, as broad and tall as a lilac-bush, its firm, glossy leaves of the deepest green and its splendid red flowers covering it from tip to sod, one specimen showing by count a thousand blossoms open at once and the sod beneath innumerably starred with others already fallen. The night jasmine, in full green, was not yet in blossom but it was visibly thinking of the spring. The Chinese privet, of twenty feet stature, in perennial leaf, was saving its flowers for May. The sea-green oleander, fifteen feet high and wide drooped to the sward on four sides but hoarded its floral cascade for June. The evergreen loquat (locally miscalled the mespilus plum) was already faltering into bloom; also the orange, with its flower-buds among its polished leaves, whitening for their own wedding; while high over them towered the date and other palms, spired the cedar and arborvitæ, and with majestic infrequency, where grounds were ample, spread the lofty green, scintillating boughs of the magnolia grandiflora the giant, winter-bare pecan and the wide, mossy arms of the vast live-oak.

Now while the time of year in which these conditions are visible heightens their lovely wonder, their practical value to Northern home-lovers is not the marvel and delight of something inimitable but their inspiring suggestion of what may be done with ordinary Northern home grounds, to the end that the floral pageantry of the Southern January may be fully rivalled by the glory of the Northern June.

For of course the Flora of the North, who in the winter of long white nights puts off all her jewelry and nearly all her robes and "lies down to pleasant dreams," is the blonde sister of, and equal heiress with, this darker one who, in undivested greenery and flowered trappings, persists in open-air revelry through all the months from the autumn side of Christmas to the summer side of

Easter. Wherefore it seems to me the Northern householder's first step should be to lay hold upon this New Orleans idea in gardening—which is merely by adoption a New Orleans idea, while through and through, except where now and then its votaries stoop to folly, it is by book a Northern voice, the garden gospel of Frederick Law Olmsted.

Wherever American homes are assembled we may have, all winter, for the asking—if we will but ask ourselves instead of the lawn-mower man—an effect of home, of comfort, cheer and grace, of summer and autumn reminiscences and of spring's anticipations, immeasurably better than any ordinary eye or fancy can extort from the rectangular and stiffened-out nakedness of unplanted boundaries; immeasurably better than the month-by-month daily death-stare of shroud-like snow around houses standing barefooted on the frozen ground. It may be by hearty choice that we abide where we must forego outdoor roses in Christmas week and broad-leaved evergreens blooming at New Year's, Twelfth-night or Carnival. Well and good! But we can have even in mid-January, and ought to allow ourselves, the lawn-garden's surviving form and tranced life rather than the shrubless lawn's unmarked grave flattened beneath the void of the snow. We ought to retain the sleeping beauty of the ordered garden's unlost configuration, with the warm house for its bosom, with all its remoter contours—alleys, bays, bushy networks and sky-line—keeping a winter share of their feminine grace and softness. We ought to retain the "frozen music" of its myriad gray, red and yellow stems and twigs and lingering blue and scarlet berries stirring, though leaflessly, for the kiss of spring. And we ought to retain the invincible green of cedars, junipers and box, cypress, laurel, hemlock spruce and cloaking ivy, darkling amid and above these, receiving from and giving to them a cheer which neither could have in their frostbound Eden without mutual contrast.

Eden! If I so recklessly ignore latitude as to borrow the name of the first gardener's garden for such a shivering garden as this it is because I see this one in a dream of hope—a diffident, interrogating hope—really to behold, some day, this dream-garden of Northern winters as I have never with actual open eyes found one kept by any merely well-to-do American citizen. If I describe it I must preface with all the disclaimers of a self-conscious amateur whose most venturesome argument goes no farther than "Why not?" yet whom the evergreen gardens of New Orleans revisited in January impel to protest against every needless submission to the tyrannies of frost and of a gardening art—or non-art, a submission which only in the outdoor embellishment of the home takes winter supinely, abjectly.

This garden of a hope's dream covers but three ordinary town lots. Often it shrinks to but one without asking for any notable change of plan. Following all the lines, the hard, law lines, that divide it from its neighbors and the street, there runs, waist-high on its street front, shoulder-high on its side bounds, a close evergreen hedge of hemlock spruce. In its young way this hedge has been handsome from infancy; though still but a few years old it gives, the twelvemonth round, a note both virile and refined in color, texture and form, and if the art that planted it and the care that keeps it do not decay neither need the hedge for a century to come. Against the intensest cold this side of Labrador it is perfectly hardy, is trimmed with a sloping top to shed snows whose weight might mutilate it, and can be kept in repair from generation to generation, like the house's plumbing or roof, or like some green-uniformed pet regiment with ranks yet full after the last of its first members has perished.

Furthermore, along the inner side of this green hedge (sometimes close against it, sometimes with a turfed alley between), as well as all round about the house, extend borders of deciduous shrubs, with such meandering boundaries next the broad white lawn as the present writer, for this time, has probably extolled enough. These bare, gray shrub masses are not wholly bare or gray and have other and most pleasingly visible advantages over unplanted, pallid vacancy, others besides the mere lace-work of their twigs and the occasional tenderness of a last summer's bird's nest. Here and there, breaking the cold monotone, a bush of moose maple shows the white-streaked green of its bare stems and sprays, or cornus or willow gives a soft glow of red, purple or yellow. Only here and there, insists my dream, lest when winter at length gives way to the "rosy time of the year" their large and rustic gentleness mar the nuptial revels of summer's returned aristocracy. Because, moreover, there is a far stronger effect of life, home and cheer from the broad-leaved evergreens which, in duly limited numbers, assemble with and behind these, and from the lither sorts of conifers that spire out of the network and haze of living things in winter sleep. The plantings at the garden's and dwelling's front being properly, of course, lower than those farther back, I see among them, in this dream, the evergreen box and several kinds of evergreen ferns. I see two or three species of evergreen barberries, not to speak of Thunberg's leafless one warm red with its all-winter berries, the winter garden's rubric. I see two varieties of euonymus; various low junipers; two sorts of laurel; two of andromeda, and the high-clambering evergreen ivy. Beginning with these in front, infrequent there but multiplying toward the place's rear, are bush and tree forms of evergreen holly, native rhododendrons, the many sorts of foreign cedars and our native ones white and red, their skyward lines modified as the square or pointed architecture of the house may call for contrasts in pointed or broad-topped arborescence. If, at times, I dream behind all this a grove, with now and then one of its broad, steepling or columnar trees pushed forward upon the lawn, it is only there that I see anything so stalwart as a pine or so rigid as a spruce.

Such is the vision, and if I never see it with open eyes and in real sunlight, even as a dream it is—like certain other things of less dignity—grateful, comforting. I warrant there are mistakes in it, but you will find mistakes wherever you find achievement, and there is no law against them—in well-meant dreams. Observe, if you please, this vision lays no drawback on the garden's summer beauty and affluence. Twelve months of the year it enhances its dignity and elegance. Both the numerical proportions of evergreens to other greens, and the scheme of their distribution, are quite as correct and effective for contrast and background to the transient foliage and countless flowers of July as amid the bare ramage of January. Summer and winter alike, the gravest items among them all, the conifers, retain their values even in those New Orleans gardens. When we remember that in New England and on all its isotherm it is winter all that half of the year when most of us are at home, why should we not seek to realize this snow-garden dream? Even a partial or faulty achievement of it will surely look lovelier than the naked house left out on its naked white lawn like an unclaimed trunk on a way-station platform. I would not, for anything, offend the reader's dignity, but I must think that this midwinter garden may be made at least as much lovelier than no garden as Alice's Cheshire cat was lovelier—with or without its grin—than the grin without the cat.

Shall we summarize? Our gist is this: that those gardens of New Orleans are as they are, not by mere advantage of climate but for several other reasons. Their bounds of ownership and privacy are enclosed in hedges, tight or loose, or in vine-clad fences or walls. The lawn is regarded as a ruling feature of the home's visage, but not as its whole countenance—one flat feature never yet made a lovely face. This lawn feature is beautified and magnified by keeping it open from shrub border to shrub border, saving it, above all things, from the gaudy barbarism of pattern-bedding; and by giving it swing and sweep of graceful contours. And lastly, all ground lines of the house are clothed with shrubberies whose deciduous growths are companioned with broad-leafed evergreens and varied conifers, in whatever proportions will secure the best midwinter effects without such abatement to those of summer as would diminish the total of the whole year's joy.

These are things that can be done anywhere in our land, and wherever done with due regard to soil as well as to climate will give us gardens worthy to be named with those of New Orleans, if not, in some aspects and at particular times of the year, excelling them. As long as mistakes are made in the architecture of houses they will be made in the architecture of gardening, and New Orleans herself, by a little more care for the fundamentals of art, of all art, could easily surpass her present floral charm. Yet in her gardens there is one further point calling for approval and imitation: the very high trimming of the stems of lofty trees. Here many a reader will feel a start of resentment; but in the name of the exceptional beauty one may there see resulting from the practice let us allow the idea a moment's entertainment, put argument aside and consider a concrete instance whose description shall be our closing word.

Across the street in which, that January, we sojourned (we were two), there was a piece of ground of an ordinary town square's length and somewhat less breadth. It had been a private garden. Its owner had given it to the city. Along its broad side, which our windows looked out upon, stood perfectly straight and upright across the sky to the south of them a row of magnolias (grandiflora) at least sixty feet high, with their boles, as smooth as the beach, trimmed bare for two-thirds of their stature. The really decorative marks of the trimming had been so many years, so many decades, healed as to show that no harm had come of it or would come. The soaring, dark-green, glittering foliage stood out against the almost perpetually blue and white sky. Beyond them, a few yards within the place but not in a straight line, rose even higher a number of old cedars similarly treated and offering a pleasing contrast to the magnolias by the feathery texture of their dense sprays and the very different cast of their lack-lustre green. Overtopping all, on the farther line of the grounds, southern line, several pecan-trees of nearly a hundred feet in height, leafless, with a multitude of broad-spreading boughs all high in air by natural habit, gave an effect strongly like that of winter elms, though much enlivened by the near company of the evergreen masses of cedar and magnolia. These made the upper-air half of the garden, the other half being assembled below. For the lofty trim of the wintergreen-trees—the beauty of which may have been learned from the palms—allowed and invited another planting beneath them. Magnolias, when permitted to branch low, are, to undergrowth, among the most inhospitable of trees, but in this garden, where the sunlight and the breezes passed abundantly under such high-lifted arms and among such clean, bare stems, a congregation of shrubs, undershrubs and plants of every stature and breadth, arose, flourished and flowered without stint. Yonder the wind-split, fathom-long leaves of the banana, brightening the background, arched upward, drooped again and faintly oscillated to the air's caress. Here bloomed and smelled the delicate magnolia fuscata, and here, redder with flowers than green with shining leaves, shone the camellia. Here spread the dark oleander, the pittosporum and the Chinese privet; and here were the camphor-tree and the slender sweet olive—we have named them all before and our steps should not take us over the same ground twice in one circuit; that would be bad gardening. But there they were, under those ordinarily so intolerant trees, prospering and singing praises with them, some in full blossom and perfume, some waiting their turn, like parts of a choir. In the midst of all, where a broad path eddied quite round an irregular open space, and that tender quaintness of decay appeared which is the unfailing New Orleans touch, the space was filled with roses. This spot was lovely enough by day and not less so for being a haunt of toddling babes and their nurses; but at night—! Regularly at evening there comes into the New Orleans air, from Heaven knows whither, not a mist, not a fog nor a dampness, but a soft, transparent, poetical dimness that in no wise shortens the range of vision—a counterpart of that condition which so many thousands of favored travellers in other longitudes know as the "Atlantic haze." One night—oh, oftener than that, but let us say one for the value of understatement—returning to our quarters some time before midnight, we stepped out upon the balcony to gaze across into that garden. The sky was clear, the neighborhood silent. A wind stirred, but the shrubberies stood motionless. The moon, nearly full, swung directly before us, pouring its gracious light through the tenuous cross-hatchings of the pecans, nestling it in the dense tops of the cedars and magnolias and sprinkling it to the ground among the lower growths and between their green-black shadows. When in a certain impotence of rapture we cast about in our minds for an adequate comparison—where description in words seemed impossible—the only parallel we could find was the art of Corot and such masters from the lands where the wonderful pictorial value of trees trimmed high has been known for centuries and is still cherished. For without those trees so disciplined the ravishing picture of that garden would have been impossible.

Of course our Northern gardens cannot smile like that in winter. But they need not perish, as tens of thousands of lawn-mower, pattern-bed, so-called gardens do. They should but hibernate, as snugly as the bear, the squirrel, the bee; and who that ever in full health of mind and body saw spring come back to a Northern garden of blossoming trees, shrubs and undershrubs has not rejoiced in a year of four clear-cut seasons? Or who that ever saw mating birds, greening swards, starting violets and all the early flowers loved of Shakespeare, Milton, Shelley, Bryant and Tennyson, has not felt that the resurrection of landscape and garden owes at least half its glory to the long trance of winter, and wished that dwellers in Creole lands might see New England's First of June? For what says the brave old song-couplet of New England's mothers? That—

> "Spring would be but wintry weather
> If we had nothing else but spring."

Every year, even in Massachusetts—even in Michigan—spring, summer, and autumn are sure to come overladen with their gifts and make us a good, long, merry visit. All the other enlightened and well-to-do nations of the world entertain them with the gardening art and its joys and so make fairer, richer and stronger than can be made indoors alone the individual soul, the family, the social, the civic, the national life. In this small matter we Americans are at the wrong end of the procession. What shall we do about it?

www.ingramcontent.com/pod-product-compliance
Lightning Source LLC
Chambersburg PA
CBHW011803040426
42450CB00017B/3450